Relations Between Africans, African Americans and Afro-Caribbeans: Tensions, Indifference and Harmony

Godfrey Mwakikagile

Copyright (c) 2007 Godfrey Mwakikagile
All rights reserved.

Relations Between Africans, African Americans and Afro-Caribbeans

First Edition

ISBN 978-0-9802587-4-5

No part of this book may be reproduced in any form for commercial purposes without written permission from the publisher.

New Africa Press
Dar es Salaam, Tanzania
Pretoria, South Africa

New Africa Press

Our books focus on the African world. They are intended for members of the general public and the academic community.

We cover a wide of range of subjects, reflected by the diversity of our titles, with primary emphasis on trade books. Academic works published by New Africa Press are also intended for the general public. Few titles, if any, are published exclusively for members of the academic community.

All our works are non-fiction addressing contemporary issues, history, politics, economics, international affairs relating to Africa, and many other subjects. People of African descent in the diaspora are an integral part of the African world and the focus of some of our works.

Because of the wide range of subjects we cover, some of our titles may not seem to be relevant to Africa and the African diaspora.. But many of our readers will find them to be useful if for no other reason than that their experience is human experience and the diversity reflected by our works derives its legitimacy from our identity as an integral part of humanity.

Contents

Acknowledgements

Introduction

Chapter One:
African Independence and Its Impact on the Struggle for Racial Equality in the United States

Chapter Two:
Africans, African Americans and Afro-Caribbeans

Chapter Three:
Relations Between Africans and Afro-Caribbeans in Britain

Chapter Four:
Africans and Afro-Caribbeans in Britain: In Their Own Words

Appendix I:
Chilly Coexistence:
Africans and African Americans in the Bronx

**Appendix II:
Contemporary African Immigrants to the United States**

**Appendix III:
Afro-Caribbeans in Britain**

About the Author

Acknowledgements

I WISH to express my profound gratitude to the people and institutions whose material I have used in this book.

I am also grateful to the members of the African, African American and Afro-Caribbean communities for being a source of inspiration in this study.

But I must also state that I felt it was my responsibility, as much it is of others, to address the subjects I have in this book because I a member of one of those groups myself.

I am an African, born and brought up in Africa. But I have also lived in the West for many years and have been able to interact with many people in the African diaspora and in the African immigrant communities in the West. All this has enabled me to acquire first-hand knowledge of the subjects I have covered in this book.

But the secondary sources I have used have been indispensable in the execution of this project. Without them, I would not have been able to complete this study the way I have and the book I would have written would have been different from this one.

This is a collective enterprise in terms of documentation. Therefore all the faults which may be found in this book are not entirely mine! But the analysis is mine. And for that I am fully responsible.

Introduction

THIS WORK looks at relations between Africans, African Americans and Afro-Caribbeans.

My previous work on this subject focused on relations between Africans and African Americans. But I knew that the study would not be complete or comprehensive without including Afro-Caribbeans who are also known as West Indians.

I have used the terms "Afro-Caribbeans" and "West Indians," sometimes interchangeably in appropriate contexts, for identification purposes as much as I have the term "black American" for the same reason.

I have also used the term "West Indians" probably more than I have "black Americans" because a very large number of black people from the Caribbean still call themselves, and many of them prefer to be called, "West Indians" instead of being called "Afro-Caribbeans" for reasons I have given in the book.

Whatever the case, we must be brutally frank that problems exist in relations between these groups, although it must also be acknowledged that many people from all these communities get along very well.

Where there are no tensions or cooperation – or much interaction – relations between many members of these groups can probably best be described as indifference towards each other rather than overt or covert hostility.

Still there are many who clash. And tensions between some groups, for example between Jamaicans and Nigerians in Britain, are a problem that needs to be addressed in order to find ways to achieve harmony.

There is also rivalry between these groups in a number areas in spite of the unity that exists among a large number of them in the United States, Britain and elsewhere.

Those are some of the subjects addressed in this book.

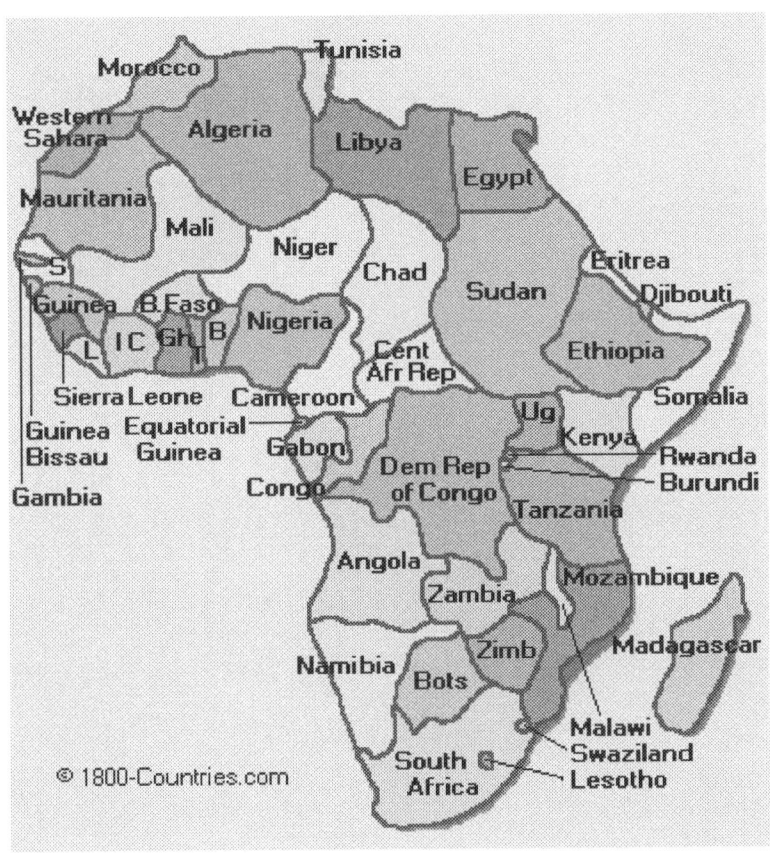

Chapter One:

African Independence and Its Impact on the Struggle for Racial Equality in the United States

THE EMERGENCE of African countries on the international scene as sovereign nations after winning independence had a profound impact on the civil rights movement in the United States.

For the first time in modern history, a large number of black countries had a voice of their own in the international arena, and also provided inspiration to the struggle for racial equality in the United States.

They also became a source of pride for millions of black Americans. Their identification with Africa was no longer something they could be ashamed of, at least for a large number of them; and the victory of their brethren in Africa was also seen as their victory.

Even before African countries emerged from colonial rule, the struggle for racial equality in the United States was inextricably linked with the independence struggle in Africa. Not only were they inextricably linked; they reinforced each other. And they had the same goals: equality and justice.

But there was one fundamental difference. While Africans were fighting for independence from colonial rule imposed on them by foreign powers, in order to rule themselves, black people in the United States were fighting for inclusion on the basis of equality with the dominant white race in the same country where they lived and the only one they knew as home. They were not fighting for independence or to have a country of their own where they could rule themselves like their brethren in Africa.

The first black African country to win independence was Ghana in 1957, followed by Guinea in 1958. And it had great symbolic significance to many black Americans in two fundamental respects. The person who led Ghana to independence, Kwame Nkrumah, went to school in the United States. Not only did he go to school in America; he went to a black school.

He attended Lincoln University in Pennsylvania, one of the most prominent historically black colleges in the United States. He also preached in black churches in Pennsylvania and New York, cementing his ties with African Americans. And his social life included dating black American girls.

The independence of Ghana was also significant to black Americans because many of their ancestors came from there when they were taken as slaves. And Nkrumah was very much aware of the significance of those ties. As he stated in his speech at a state dinner on Ghana's independence day on 6 March 1957:

> There exists a firm bond of sympathy between us and the Negro peoples of the Americas. The ancestors of so many of them come from this country. Even today in the West Indies, it is possible to hear words and phrases which come from various languages of the Gold Coast. - (Kwame Nkrumah, *I Speak of Freedom: A Statement of African Ideology*, New York: Praeger, 1961, p. 96).

And during Ghana's independence celebrations, Nkrumah invited many African Americans to Accra, Ghana's capital, to participate. Some of those who went were ordinary citizens including a teacher from California who got a personal invitation from Nkrumah after she wrote him saying she wanted to participate in Ghana's independence celebrations in Accra.

Among the prominent African Americans invited were Dr. Martin Luther King and his deputy Ralph Abernathy; UN Undersecretary-General Dr. Ralph Bunche; veteran civil rights leader A. Philip Randolph; and Harlem Congressman Adam Clayton Powell who was also pastor of the Abyssinian Baptist Church in Harlem which Nkrumah visited when he was a student at Columbia University in New York.

One year after Ghana's independence, Nkrumah went to the United States at the invitation of President Dwight Eisenhower. He was then prime minister of Ghana, not president, since the country was not yet a republic.

He used the occasion to reflect on his student days in the United States and on the close ties he had with African Americans whose school he also attended. As he stated in his book, *I Speak of Freedom* (p. 135), his first visit to the United States as the prime minister of Ghana after leading his country to independence was, in a sense, "the fulfilment of the hopes and dreams of my student days at Lincoln University."

Among the places he visited when he was in the United States as the official guest of President Eisenhower in 1958 was Harlem. Nkrumah recalled the visit in his book *I Speak of Freedom* (p. 145) with pride and affection in the following terms: "The spectacular and spontaneous welcome given to me by the people of Harlem remains one of the happiest memories of the whole tour."

Nkrumah again visited Harlem in the spring of 1961. This time his official title was President of the Republic of Ghana. The Ghanaian parliament adopted a new constitution and voted in March 1960 to transform Ghana into a republic.

During his visit to Harlem in 1961, Nkrumah further strengthened his ties with Black America and addressed a rally in Harlem and reminded his audience that he used to live in Harlem during his student days.

When he was a student at the University of Pennsylvania, he spent summers in New York City and sold fish in the streets of Harlem which is predominantly black and an integral part of New York City. He also lived in Harlem when he was a student at Columbia University, a predominantly white school which is also in Harlem.

During his student days, Nkrumah also worked in a soap factory, which affected his health, and served as a waiter on merchant ships plying the coastlines of the United States and Central America to earn enough money to go to school and support himself.

Nkrumah never forgot those days. They were hard times. But they were also good times in terms of forging and strengthening ties with black Americans some of whom could, in fact., have been his blood relatives since many of the ancestors of black Americans came from Ghana.

And when he visited Harlem, twice, his presence in this predominantly black district as president of an African country symbolized a victory the people of Harlem could identify with and celebrate. They saw him as one of their own, which he was.

His visit to Harlem was also during a time when the civil rights movement in the United States was gaining momentum, drawing inspiration from Ghana's victory in its struggle for independence and from the victory of other black African countries which attained sovereign status during that period.

Ghana's, and Africa's, ties to Black America assumed more significance only three years later when Ghana's ambassador to the United Nations, Alex Quaison-Sackey, became the first black person to be elected president of the UN General Assembly in December 1964.

He regarded his election not only as the fulfilment of the African personality – a concept forcefully articulated by Nkrumah - but also as "a tribute to Africa, and to Ghana in particular and to millions of people of African descent everywhere."

His election was widely celebrated and received a lot of coverage in African newspapers including the *Ghanaian Times*, 2 and 3 December 1964.

And in his book *Africa Unbound* (pp. 35 – 58) published in 1963, Quaison-Sackey has an entire chapter devoted to a discussion of the concept of the African personality.

He later became Ghana's minister of foreign affairs and held that position when Nkrumah was overthrown months later on 24 February 1966 in a coup engineered and masterminded by the CIA.

Tragically, the coup was facilitated by the black American ambassador to Ghana, Franklin Williams, who was also Nkrumah's classmate at Lincoln University. Nkrumah never forgot that and even wrote about it in his book *Dark Days in Ghana* on the military coup.

In spite of this setback, Nkrumah remained a symbol of African independence and dignity and the most prominent spokesman for the black race since Marcus Garvey. In December

1999, BBC listeners in Africa voted Kwame Nkrumah the "Man of the Millennium."And he blazed the trail for the African independence movement. As he said in his speech on Ghana's independence day, 6 March 1957:

> We are going to see that we create our own African identity and personality. We again rededicate ourselves in the struggle to emancipate other countries in Africa; for, our independence is meaningless unless it is linked up with the total liberation of the African continent.

Even when he was a still student in the United States, he stood out among other students as a strong advocate for black freedom and had a strong interest not only in African history but also in black American history and culture. He even wrote a "Negro history"series for the student newspaper at Lincoln University and taught classes on the subject at the University of Pennsylvania.

He also learnt as much as he could about civil rights organizations in the United States including the NAACP and the Urban League.

All that helped to strengthen his ties with Black America during the struggle for Ghana's independence and when he became president of his country probably best symbolized by his invitation to Dr. W.E.B. DuBois to go to Ghana and direct the Encyclopedia Africana project. DuBois was not only the pre-eminent intellectual in the American civil rights struggle since the early 1900s; he was also a prominent advocate of African independence and wrote books about Africa.

Although there were two independent countries in sub-Saharan Africa before Ghana won independence in 1957, they did not have the status Ghana had after the former British colony of the Gold Coast emerged from colonial rule and became Ghana.

The two countries were Ethiopia and Liberia, both with dubious credentials as black independent countries but for different reasons. Ethiopia was never colonized, except for a brief occupation by the Italians from 1935 - 1941. Therefore it did not have to fight for independence. And the Italian invaders were expelled by the Allied forces in 1941.

Ethiopia also had dubious credentials as a black country since most Ethiopians are not "Negroes" and many of them don't identify with black Africa because of their different racial identity, although a significant number of them also call themselves black but still with some distinctions.

Many of them say they are black but not "Negro," which is true. By remarkable contrast, most African countries in sub-Saharan are inhabited by people who are collectively identified as members of the same "black race" and same origin.

In the case of Liberia also, as in the case of Ethiopia, the struggle for independence was not part of its history. Liberia was founded by the American Colonization Society in 1822 as a home for freed American slaves. Therefore it did not have to fight for independence from a foreign colonial power the way Ghana and other African countries did.

In terms of racial identity and credentials as a nation representative of black Africa or the black race, Liberia is a predominantly black country like Ghana and most of the other countries in sub-Saharan Africa. And it became a republic in 1847 but virtually remained an American colony.

It has sometimes been called America's "51st state." Firestone, an American company, which dominated the economy was the *de facto* ruler of Liberia. And the country is still dominated by the United States today.

So it was not until Ghana emerged on the scene as an independent country that a new chapter in the history of black colonial Africa was written. Ghana not only fought for independence; it also won independence from a foreign power becoming the first black nation in sub-Saharan Africa to emerge from colonial rule, a victory that had a profound emotional and psychological impact on the struggle for racial equality in the United States.

Nkrumah's quest for continental unification under one government also had strong emotional and rhetorical appeal among many people in Africa and blacks in the United States who knew that Africa was weak because it was not united, among other reasons; and Black America was also weak because it was not as united as it should be, although the minority status of black people in a predominantly white society was probably an even bigger problem in the American context.

Nkrumah's ambition to unite African countries under one government may have been dismissed by many people as a

Utopian ideal but it inspired many others and future generations to work towards continental unity and racial solidarity across continents to embrace blacks in the United States and other people of African descent in other parts of the world. As he stated in his book *I Speak of Freedom*:

> Divided we are weak; united, Africa could become one of the greatest forces for good in the world.
> I believe strongly and sincerely that with the deep-rooted wisdom and dignity, the innate respect for human lives, the intense humanity that is our heritage, the African race, united under one federal government, will emerge not as just another world bloc to flaunt its wealth and strength, but as a Great Power whose greatness is indestructible because it is built not on fear, envy and suspicion, nor won at the expense of others, but founded on hope, trust, friendship and directed to the good of all mankind.

Nkrumah's message reverberated across the Atlantic and elsewhere. It was a message of hope, redemption and racial solidarity, and it resonated well among blacks in the United States in their quest for racial equality as much as it did wherever oppressed people, especially black people, were fighting for freedom.

Ironically, it was the oppressors themselves who facilitated the struggle for racial equality in the United States and the independence struggle in Africa. Some of their policies and decisions had unintended consequences. One of those developments was the involvement if the imperial powers, and the United States, in World War II.

And one of the most important outcomes of the war was the fundamental change that took place in the relationship between whites – the rulers of the world – and non-whites including blacks.

The relationship between the races, which was of an asymmetrical nature, was never to be the same again. As Dr. W.E.B. DuBois stated prophetically in the early 1900s in his book *Souls of Black Folk*: "The problem of the twentieth century is the problem of the colour line – the relation of the darker to the lighter races of man in Asia and Africa, in America and the islands of the sea."

Africans and Asians were no longer going to tolerate their subordinate position as colonial subjects after the war in which they had fought to free others and keep the world "safe for democracy." And black people in the United States were not going to continue living as second-class citizens in the land of their birth and saw their struggle as inextricably linked with the struggle for justice and racial equality throughout the world. Many of them, like their African brethren, fought and died in World War II when the United States joined the Allied forces to fight Hitler and other enemies of freedom and racial equality; ironically while the United States itself did not allow its own black citizens to enjoy racial equality whites always took for granted throughout their lives.

Black people were determined to fight for their rights. They had already sacrificed so much in World War II fighting for the freedom of others, and they were not going to stop fighting. As Dr. DuBois stated, "We went fighting, we came back fighting."

The struggle for racial equality in the United States intensified during the same decade when the majority of African countries won independence. At no time in American history was the campaign against segregation and discrimination as sustained as it was in the sixties. And it was no longer a domestic problem. It assumed another dimension as a part of a global struggle by oppressed and non-white peoples to reclaim their status as equals in a world that was dominated by whites.

The United States was fully aware of this changed international situation. And it had a profound impact on America's standing in the global arena. Here was a country which, as the citadel of democracy, portrayed itself as a beacon of hope and source of inspiration for oppressed people around the world. Yet it denied some of its citizens the very same rights it claimed to cherish so much. Black people were denied not only democratic rights; they were also denied human rights. The establishment, and the vast majority of whites, refused to accept them as equal human beings.

America's enemies including the Soviet Union used it as a powerful weapon against the United States, accusing her of hypocrisy, although the Soviets themselves and other critics of America were oppressing their own people.

But they never claimed to be great democrats the way Americans did. And there were, of course, countries which were indeed democratic and had the higher moral ground in their criticism of the United States.

The emergence of African countries as independent countries also enabled them to articulate a position that showed them as champions of equality and justice for all people regardless of race. They had just emerged from colonial rule under which they were oppressed and exploited and were now not only being looked up to by black Americans as a source of inspiration in the struggle for racial equality in the United States; they themselves were speaking up against racial injustice everywhere, including the United States, having been victims of racial injustice themselves.

At the founding of the Organization of African Unity (OAU), the African heads of state and government issued a statement condemning racism in the United States.

Therefore there is no question that continental Africans have shown great interest in the civil rights struggle in the United States.

During the civil rights movement, African governments took strong interest in the struggle for racial equality in the United States and issued a formal statement which not only condemned racial injustice against people of African descent in the United States; it virtually amounted to saying America was being hypocritical when it portrayed itself as the custodian of human and democratic rights worthy of emulation by other nations round the globe.

The statement was in the form of a resolution linking racial discrimination in the United States with apartheid in South Africa and was issued by the African heads of state and government who met in Addis Ababa, Ethiopia, in May 1963, to form the Organization of African Unity. And it was incorporated into the OAU Charter:

> The Summit Conference of Independent African States meeting in Addis Ababa, Ethiopia, from 22 May to 25 May 1963; having considered all aspects of the questions of apartheid and racial discriminations; unanimously convinced of the imperious and urgent necessity of co-ordinating and intensifying their efforts to put an end to the South African Government's criminal policy of apartheid and wipe out racial discrimination in all its forms,...(also) expresses the deep concern aroused in all African peoples and governments by the measures of racial discrimination taken against communities of African origin living outside the continent and particularly in

the United States of America,...intolerable mal-practices which are likely seriously to deteriorate relations between the African peoples and governments on the one hand and the people and Government of the United States of America on the other.

And in the following year, after the OAU summit of African heads of state and government met in Cairo, Egypt, in July (1964), African leaders addressed the subject of racial discrimination in the United States.

That was after Malcolm X spoke at the conference and appealed to African leaders to raise the matter at the United Nations. If apartheid in South Africa could be addressed by the UN, he saw no reason why racial discrimination against people of African descent in the United States could not be accorded the same treatment.

About nine African countries including Ghana, Guinea, Tanzania, Mali and Egypt agreed to take up the matter and bring it before the UN General Assembly but did not do so for a number of reasons including diplomatic and political problems and strong opposition from the United States government.

When Malcolm X went on a trip to several African countries in July 1964, State Department officials in Washington complained about his activities, saying he was causing a lot of trouble for the United States in Africa where he also strongly condemned American involvement in the Congo and in the assassination of Patrice Lumumba.

And the assassination of Malcolm X himself several months later on February 21, 1965, after his African trip, sealed the fate of this subject since he was the only major African American leader who consistently worked to have it brought before the UN.

His assassination was condemned by many people in Africa and was the subject of discussion in different circles, including the media, as were other assassinations during that period in Africa and in the United States as well, including Lumumba's and President John Kennedy's. American intervention in the Congo was also bitterly condemned in African countries and at the United Nations by African diplomats and representatives from many other countries.

The United States drew sharp criticism especially when it supported Tshombe and when, in November 1964 together with

Belgium, it sent troops to Stanleyville, the stronghold of Lumumba's supporters, ostensibly to rescue westerners – including missionary workers – who were "trapped" there. The result was a massacre of thousands of innocent black Congolese. As the *Ghanaian Times* stated on 28 November 1964:

> After killing thousands to free their few spies, the Americans and Belgians stayed on to aid the already entrenched mercenaries to exterminate Congolese citizens in an effort to reintegrate Stanleyville into the Leopoldville administration.

And on 26 February 1965, five days after Malcolm X was assassinated on February 21st in New York City, a vitriolic condemnation of the United States graced the pages of *The Spark*, a political journal of Ghana's ruling Convention People's Party (CPP) led by Dr. Nkrumah and which declared itself to be "A Socialist Weekly of the African Revolution."

In an article entitled "Who Killed Malcolm X, a Negro American," W.G. Smith accused the "leaders of fascist imperialism who control the invisible government of the United States" of killing not only Malcolm X but also Lumumba, Kennedy, the prime minister of Burundi and three high-ranking officials in the government of Congo-Brazzaville.

The writer – or presumed author who could have been writing under a pen name and may even have been a Ghanaian government official or an intelligence officer - also accused the United States of bombing Uganda and North Vietnam and of plotting to overthrow the government of Tanzania and sabotage its pro-African revolutionary policies.

He also accused the United States of overthrowing the government of Sudan and collaborating with what he described as the South African Nazis in slaughtering the Congolese people. As he also stated: "The death lashes of the imperialist monster, in its long drawn out agony, are sometimes terrible."

And in an accompanying editorial, *The Spark* accused the American ruling class of assassinating Malcolm X because nine African countries, influenced by Malcolm X, were going to bring up the issue of racial discrimination in the United States at the United Nations to have it discussed in the General Assembly. As the editorial went on to say: "Even a member of their own class, like the millionaire Kennedy, is rubbed out because he evinced the slightest desire for changing the tactics of American foreign and military strategy."

The interest of African countries in what was happening in the United States was two-fold. As a superpower, whatever the United States did affected the entire world, Africa being no exception. And as home to millions of people of African descent, the United States had a direct impact on the fate of black people everywhere because oppression of one segment of the black race - as was happening in the United States where black people did not have equal rights enjoyed by whites – affected the entire race, hence Africa itself.

And while it is true that African countries and their victory when they won independence mostly in the sixties were a source of inspiration and pride to millions of African Americans in their struggle for racial equality, it is also worth remembering that black Americans had also, in years before, played a significant role in fuelling African nationalism.

They were among the founders of the Pan-African movement whose ideology of Pan-Africanism highly inspired future African leaders such as Nkrumah, Azikiwe, and Nyerere in Anglophone Africa. And they continued to support the independence struggle across the continent through the years.

The emergence of African countries on the global scene as sovereign entities also changed America's perception of Africa. It also changed the attitude many black Americans had towards their ancestral homeland.

Shame was replaced with pride among many blacks in the United States. And where there was ambivalence, even if not necessarily a negative attitude towards Africa, now prevailed a positive attitude unequivocally defensive of their ancestral origin. There was also a sense of racial solidarity with a people once considered primitive and incapable of helping themselves.

The achievement of independence by African countries played a major role in changing these attitudes among many – probably the majority – of black Americans.

Fuelling African nationalism – as well as Asia's – and identification with Black America and vice versa was the assumption by white powers, even if not explicitly or crudely expressed the way Nazi Germany did under Hitler, that the subordination of non-whites was a natural development. The implication of this was that it was ordained by God in a world based on a hierarchy of the races, and in which only white nations had the divine mandate to rule.

But the emergence of African and Asian nations on the international scene as sovereign entities especially after the end of World War II not only challenged that assumption to the core; it shattered the myth of white racial superiority that had been nurtured for so long in a world where imperial domination neatly coincided with skin colour.

In the case of Africa, such domination was bolstered not only by the doctrine of white supremacy but by the perceived "inferiority"of black people as the most backward, and least intelligent, among all the races. They had "inferior" genes and were on the lowest rung of the evolutionary ladder! As Sir Godfrey Huggins, prime minister of Southern Rhodesia, once said at press conference in London:

> There would be no Africans in a federal government (of the Federation of Rhodesia and Nyasaland). They are quite incapable of playing a full part....They may have a university degree, but their background is all wrong.
>
> It is time for the people in England to realize that the white man in Africa is not prepared and never will be prepared to accept the African as an equal, either socially or politically.
>
> Is there something in their chromosomes which makes them more backward and different from peoples living in the East and West? - (Godfrey Huggins, quoted by Colin M. Turnbull, *The Lonely African*, New York: Simon & Schuster, 1962, p. 90).

This is a man who was acclaimed as a British liberal yet harboured some of the most racist, and most offensive, notions about black people.

Black people in the United States had also endured such racial taunts and insults, and much more including lynchings, for centuries – for no other reason than that they were an African people. And when their brethren in Africa demanded and won independence and began to rule themselves, the victory against imperial rule undermined all rationale that had been invoked in the United States as well to justify racial supremacy and deny blacks the rights they were entitled to as equal human beings. Like in Africa, the sixties were a defining moment. It was a decade that changed America and the destiny of Africa.

One of the immediate results of African victory over colonialism was the influx of African students and other Africans - including diplomats although in fewer numbers since there is only a limited number of diplomatic posts - into the United States soon after independence in the fifties and sixties. And they had a major impact on the domestic scene.

American authorities were careful in the way they handled them in a society where the twin evils of segregation and discrimination were a prominent feature of national life and not just in the southern states; although segregation in northern states was much more subtle than in the south where it was even flaunted by rabid segregationists who included many local and state government officials as well as federal.

All that had unintended consequences even if only to a smaller degree in a number of cases.

But to win allies in the Third World in its competition with the Soviet Union and other communist countries including China, and to burnish its image as a democratic country, the United States established ties with the newly independent states on the African continent in many areas including education soon after they won independence.

Scholarships were offered to thousands of African students to study in the United States. And many other Africans were invited to visit the United States.

Yet by doing so, the United States was forced to improve the domestic scene in terms of race relations - at a pace it had not anticipated - so that the foreigners who were now coming into the country in even much larger numbers than they did in the past would not be subjected to indignities of racial discrimination especially in the southern states where there was overt discrimination.

The government therefore had to do a lot more to end segregation and discrimination in a way it had not done in the past. In many cases it was only of symbolic significance; for example making sure that African students who had been offered scholarships by the American government were not sent to hostile areas in the south where they would face discrimination. But the mere fact that the government was now forced to pay more attention to the problem of racial discrimination, and put the issue on the national agenda as a priority, definitely benefited black people in the United States and facilitated the struggle for racial equality.

Had African countries not won independence when they did; and had Africans not gone to the United States in large numbers as students, diplomats, tourists and so forth, the American government would probably have been slower in implementing changes that were needed to achieve racial equality. It would also not have pursued the matter seriously had the rest of the world not focused its eyes on America because of what was going on in the country.

During the civil rights movement pictures were splashed across front pages in newspapers in many countries showing black people being brutalized by the authorities for simply demanding the right to vote or to use public facilities they were not allowed to use simply because they were black. And that showed how hypocritical the United States was, professing democracy abroad while denying millions of its own citizens democracy at home simply because they were not white.

So the United States was faced with a highly sensitive issue. It was also dealing with a people or with peoples who had just emerged from colonial rule under which they were subjected to racial discrimination and humiliation in their own countries and who not tolerate anymore racial insults not just in their countries in Africa – or in Asia – but anywhere else including the United States where they were visiting or going to school. And many of them were very sensitive to racial insults and indignities, and for good reason.

When some African diplomats complained of racial discrimination on the interstate highway between New York and Washington, D.C., when they tried to use public facilities such as restaurants and restrooms, President Kennedy told State Department officials to "Tell them to fly."

And when Harlem black Congressman Adam Clayton Powell introduced a bill in Congress in May 1961 imposing stiff fines and other penalties on anyone who discriminated against foreign dignitaries including ambassadors as well as other officials and their staffs from foreign countries because of their racial identity, *The Washington Post* was quick to respond to that, chiding Congressman Powell for introducing such a bill. It is true they were being discriminated against because of their racial identity as Powell said but, as *The Washington Post* stated:

> The bill seems to assume that foreign envoys travelling in the United States are special objects of discrimination. But the fact is that they suffer discrimination only when they are mistaken for Americans.

One such victim was Komla Gbedemah, Ghana's minister of finance under Nkrumah soon after the country won independence who was also the second most powerful man in Ghana after Nkrumah himself.

The discrimination he suffered when travelling from New York to Washington D.C., with his black American secretary led to an international incident.

Gbedemah himself promised the manager at the restaurant where he was denied a glass of orange juice an appropriate response and what happened was splashed in many newspapers around the world. And as Professor Thayer Watkins at San Jose State University in California stated in "The Volta River Project in Ghana":

> Nkrumah prevailed upon President Dwight Eisenhower to use his personal influence to persuade Henry Kaiser to put together a consortium of aluminum companies to build an aluminum smelter in Ghana. Kaiser and the consortium were willing to build the aluminum smelter only if the price of electricity was extremely low. Later that low price was criticized as exploitative but it had to be that low to induce the aluminum producers to build the smelter in the first place.
>
> There is an interesting anecdote concerned with how the Volta River Project was resurrected. Komla Gbedemah, the Minister of Finance and a top leader of Ghana second only to Nkrumah, was traveling in the U.S. in 1957. He and his secretary, an African American, stopped for breakfast at a roadside restaurant in Delaware and ordered orange juice. The waitress said she could not serve him because he was black. Gbedemah asked to see the manager who told him the same thing. Gbedemah then told the manager:
>
> 'The people here are of a lower social status than I am but they can drink here and we can't. You can keep the orange juice and the change, but this is not the last you have heard of this.'
>
> The next day the incident was headline news around the world. President Eisenhower invited him for breakfast the next day. Eisenhower asked

Gbedemah what he was visiting in America for and Gbedemah told him it was to try to find funding for the Volta River Dam. Eisenhower asked Vice President Richard Nixon to help arrange financing.

This incident demonstrates one simple truth, and a harsh reality, about the American racial situation. Black Africans including leaders and other non-white foreigners coming to the United States – or staying in the United States as students and diplomats – could not be accorded respect and equal treatment *unless* black Americans got the same rights and treatment whites took for granted as their natural right.

So, Africans had a direct impact on the struggle for racial equality by their mere presence in the United States. If white Americans were going to treat them with respect, they also would have to treat black Americans with respect. The fate of both as black people were inextricably linked and no amount of sophistry or clever reasoning by opponents of racial equality – some of whom may have wanted to treat Africans differently, with "respect" – could change that reality.

There was a wide gulf between what the United States preached and what it practised. It espoused lofty ideals which it rarely implemented especially in terms of democracy and race relations in the case of black Americans. All this had a direct impact on America's relations with African countries and others, prompting many delegates to the United Nations – representing non-white countries – to call for the removal of the UN headquarters from New York because of the numerous indignities African and Asian diplomats, and others, suffered in the United States because they were not white.

The American government tried to defuse tension, and placate the diplomats and other foreigners, by offering them special treatment. Yet most of them were not impressed by that and did not want any favours as long as black people in the United States did not have the same rights.

Black Americans themselves used that as a weapon in their struggle for racial equality: Why should they be denied service at restaurants, accommodation at hotels, housing and other services when foreigners - Africans and Asians - were not? After all, they were Americans, denied basic human rights in their own country which were now being offered to foreigners as a privilege.

Some black Americans even wore African attire to insulate themselves from mistreatment at the hands of whites when, for example, they walked into restaurants or tried to use restrooms and other public facilities including libraries which were off-limits to black people in the southern states. Such disguise also served to underscore one harsh reality about the United States - showing how hypocritical it was.

None of this, or very little of it, would have been possible had African countries not won independence; and had their representatives - diplomats, students, and just visitors - not gone to the United States in large numbers, thus further exposing the ugly reality of racial discrimination in a country which prides itself to be the citadel of democracy.

Therefore the American racial problem was no longer a domestic issue; it became an international issue, thrust into the international spotlight by Africans – and even by Asians - from independent countries who refused to be mistreated in the United States because of the colour of their skin; and who also refused to accept privileges or special treatment from American authorities and other whites if black Americans were not given the same rights and privileges.

So the United States had to make some concessions to accommodate black Americans as equal citizens who were entitled to the same rights whites were, although racism still remained a major problem as it still is today almost 40 years after the end of the civil rights movement which reached its peak in 1968, the same year in which Dr. Martin Luther King was assassinated. And as James Baldwin stated in *The Fire Next Time*:

> Most of the Negroes I know do not believe that this immense concession would ever have been made if it had not been for the competition of the Cold War, and the fact that Africa was clearly liberating herself and therefore had, for political reasons, to be wooed by the descendants of her former masters.
>
> Had it been a matter of love or justice, the 1954 decision [concerning school segregation] would surely have occurred sooner; were it not for the realities of power in this difficult era, it might very well not have occurred yet.
> - (James Baldwin, *The Fire Next Time*, New York, 1964, pp. 117 – 118).

There is no question that like emancipation from slavery in the 1860s which put black Americans on the road towards racial equality, the end of colonialism in Africa a century later definitely played a major role in fuelling the civil rights movement in the United States and probably in a way the white establishment had never anticipated.

Had the American rulers foreseen that, it is very much possible that they would have tried to convince the colonial powers in Africa to delay independence for Africans, knowing the liberation of black people on the African continent would have a direct impact on the racial situation in the United States which the majority of whites were not ready or prepared to change.

The emergence of African countries on the international scene as independent nations also enabled many black Americans to re-evaluate themselves not only in the American context but also in a global context the same way the Jews did following the establishment of Israel as an independent state in 1948.

The independence of Africa enhanced the stature, and status, of black Americans as a people since they could identify with the new rulers and the rest of the people in general in the new nations on the African continent. For the first time, they saw a large number of countries which – from top to bottom – were ruled and controlled by black people to whom they were related as an African people themselves; a situation analogous to the way the Jews feel about Israel as an independent Jewish state, the only one in the world.

For black Americans, their identification with Africa was also an assertion of "I am Somebody," not only in America but in the whole world by a people who had always been regarded as nonentities since their ancestors were shipped to the New World as slaves.

Their "nothingness" was forcefully articulated by Ralph Ellison when said in Harlem the reply to the greeting "How are you?" is quite often, "Oh, man, I'm nowhere." As he stated in *Shadow and Act*:

> The phrase "I'm nowhere" expresses the feeling borne in upon many Negroes that they have no stable, recognized place in society.
> One's identity drifts in a capricious reality in which even the most commonly held assumptions are questionable. One "is" literally, but one is nowhere; one wonders dazed in a ghetto maze, a "displaced person" of American democracy. - (Ralph Ellison, *Shadow and Act*, New York, 1963, p. 300).

The "nowhere-ness" or "nothingness" of black Americans was suddenly cast off by many black Americans when black Africans made a dramatic entry on the international scene as representatives and citizens of black independent countries ruled by blacks.

Even for those who were still ashamed of Africa or had an ambivalent attitude towards the homeland of their forefathers, there was a new awakening – as was the case among many whites – to a new reality in terms of how they looked at the racial identity of black people in general.

Their perception changed, transformed by the highly visible presence of black Africans in positions of authority in Africa – including presidencies – which before then since the conquest of the world by the white nations of Europe had been the exclusive monopoly of whites in most cases.

The independence of African countries had a lasting impact on Black America and on their struggle for racial equality in a country largely built by their African ancestors.

And that continued to be the case through the decades as more and more black people in the United States not only identified with Africa but sought to establish and strengthen ties with their motherland.

In the same decade in which most African countries won independence, the sixties, which was also the same decade in which the civil rights movement gained momentum and the struggle for racial equality was most intense in the United States; many American blacks made a spiritual return to Africa.

They adopted African lifestyles which included learning about different African cultures, eating African foods, wearing African clothes and learning Kiswahili and other African languages. Some of them even embraced African religions and adopted African marriage rituals and ceremonies. They also took African names to complement the African attire and lifestyles as a truly African people living and "trapped" in what some of them - such as the Black Muslims - called "the wilderness" of North America.

It was also during this period that many of them started calling themselves Afro-Americans, instead of calling themselves or being called "Negroes," to identify with a specific location as the land of their origin. As Malcolm X asked: "Where is Negroland?"

There is no such country or continent called Negroland.

It was also the same decade in which black students and professors in the United States demanded the introduction of African and Afro-American studies in colleges and universities – as well as in many high schools - across the nation.

Many of those programmes became full-fledged departments even in some of the nation's leading universities. And they continue to exist today, although in fewer numbers as the assault on black studies especially by conservative and racist forces continues unabated.

But there is no question that the introduction of African studies into the curriculum had its roots in the sixties partly because of the emergence of African countries as sovereign entities on the international scene in a decade which changed the destiny not only of the African continent but of America as well when the most comprehensive civil rights legislation was passed by Congress to guarantee racial equality for blacks in the oldest republic in the world since Rome.

The independence of African countries helped to change America and facilitate the struggle for racial equality in the United States. Black America also helped to change Africa by providing inspiration to the independence struggle on the continent and in the struggle against white minority regimes on the continent including apartheid in South Africa. As Nelson Mandela stated in his autobiography *Long Walk to Freedom*, one of the people who inspired him in the struggle against apartheid was Dr. Martin Luther King.

Not only did the two movements complement each other; they started in earnest on both sides of the Atlantic during the same period, in the fifties. They also achieved victory during the same decade, the sixties, which was hailed as Africa's decade of independence.

The civil rights movement in the United States and the African independence movement were but two sides of the same coin. And they changed world history. They were destined to.

The history of Africa is inextricably linked with the history of the United States; so are their destinies because of the presence of millions of people of African descent on American soil and without whose ancestors America would not be what it is today. It is doubtful that the United States would even have survived - let alone prospered - as a nation had it not been for the labour extracted from African slaves.

And because of these insoluble ties, it was inevitable that whatever happened in Africa in the quest for independence from foreign domination by white powers would have a direct impact on the struggle for racial equality in the United States.

It is these historical and genealogical ties which are the strongest bonds of unity between Africans and African Americans. And they continue to sustain their relationship – as much as they do in the case of other people of African descent in terms of their ties with continental Africans – although relations between many members of these groups have not always been cordial.

Sometimes those relations have been characterized by ambivalence, indifference and even hostility, overt and covert. They have also been characterized by harmony.

Those are some of the subjects addressed in the following chapters.

"All peoples of African descent whether they live in North or South America, the Caribbean or in other parts of the world, are Africans and belong to the African nation." - Kwame Nkrumah.

Chapter Two:

Africans, African Americans and Afro-Caribbeans

AFRICANS, African Americans and Afro-Caribbeans are united by their common ancestry. They are also united by their history of oppression and suffering under their European conquerors.

Yet they constitute distinct groups whose identities have been shaped by different historical experiences in different environments.

But they are all an African people, a sentiment that has been forcefully articulated by many people including prominent leaders such as Marcus Garvey, Kwame Nkrumah, Julius Nyerere, Sekou Toure, CLR James, Malcolm X, Stokely Carmichael renamed Kwame Ture and many others. As Nelson Mandela said in a speech before an African American audience in Harlem, New York, not long after he was released from prison: "We are all children of Africa."

Yet, in spite of such common identity and a common history of oppression and suffering, relations between Africans and African Americans, and between Afro-Caribbeans and African Americans as well as between Africans and Afro-Caribbeans have not always been good.

Many of them don't always see themselves as one people in spite of their common African heritage. They constitute distinct ethnic groups in countries such as the United States, Canada, Britain and the island nations in the Caribbean.

They have shared and conflicting perceptions about each other.

Those perceptions have also been shaped not only by their different historical experiences but also by their conquerors who have played a major role using various means – including miseducation and the media – to keep them divided.

The perceptions have also been shaped by other factors in contemporary times. For example, hostility towards Africans in Britain by a significant number of Afro-Caribbeans – even if muted in many cases – can be attributed to the upward mobility of a disproportionately large number of African immigrants.

Studies show that African immigrants are probably the most highly educated group in the United Kingdom surpassing the Chinese and other Asians especially from India and Pakistan who were ahead for many years and still remain some of the most highly educated people in Britain.

In addition to being the most highly educated people in Britain, surpassing not only other immigrants but also whites native to the UK, Africans are also going to be the largest ethnic group in the United Kingdom by 2010.

Already about half a million, the population of Africans in the UK has, in only a few years, surpassed that of West Indians including those of Asian origin – for example Indians from Trinidad and Jamaica – and not just Afro-Caribbeans.

According to data obtained from the 2001 census, there were 566,000 black Caribbeans by that year, and 485,000 black Africans.

Many of those Africans also have higher incomes than Afro-Caribbeans mainly because of their high education. Yet on average, even those with high education earn less than West Indians do because they are less "British" than Afro-Caribbeans in the UK and are therefore not fully accepted in British society. The result is discrimination across the spectrum.

Even new immigrants straight from the Caribbean islands which were once British colonies are considered to have been anglicized and are therefore more British than African immigrants who have lived in Britain even longer than the new arrivals from the West Indies. The new West Indian immigrants also consider themselves to be anglicized, hence more "British" than African immigrants regardless of how long these Africans have lived in Britain.

The isolation of Africans is accentuated by cultural differences and is made even worse because African immigrants retain their cultures and traditions and even pass them on to their children born and brought up in the United Kingdom. And their strong family values have helped them to maintain cohesive units and succeed in life at a rate higher than that of other black immigrants from the West Indies.

It is a disparity that not only generates, and fuels, tensions between the two groups despite their common identity as blacks and as minorities in a predominantly white society; it reinforces stereotypes about each other; it prevents them from forging alliances in pursuit of common goals and objectives; and it even affects relations between the people of both groups who don't even live in the UK.

Studies also show that African immigrants surpass other groups as well in many areas. According to a BBC report, "African Success in the UK Highlighted," 7 September 2005:

> African-born immigrants in Britain are doing better economically than many other migrants, a major new survey shows. The report (was written) by the Institute for Public Policy Research....
>
> "The Born Abroad" report showed that over half of Britain's population growth in recent years could be attributed to immigration. South Africans and Kenyans top the list of African countries included.
>
> The study, based on the national census for the 10 years up to 2001, showed that the biggest increase in migrants from Africa during the period came from Somalia and Zimbabwe.

Zimbabwe has some of the most highly educated people in Africa and in the world and many of them have settled in Britain, especially since the late nineties.

The status of African immigrants in Britain as the most highly educated group is virtually identical to their brethren in the United States where tensions also exist between Africans and African Americans for a number of other reasons as well, not just disparity in income and education between the two groups. According to the 2000 census in the United States, African immigrants had the highest income among all immigrant groups, attributed to their high education. They were also identified as the most highly educated group in the country.

Years of intermingling and even "intermarriage" between

members of these groups of African people have not broken down let alone eliminated all the barriers which divide them. They maintain their separate identities even when they live in the same communities, as many of them are forced to, because of racism. Many of them are also suspicious of each other. And their separate identities are fortified by stereotypes and misconceptions about each other and by their different historical experiences: African, American, and Afro-Caribbean.

Although many of them get along very well, there are many cases in which relations between and among the members of these groups are also characterized by tensions generated not only by misconceptions about each other but also by rivalries and cultural differences.

Even the Afro-Caribbean community is not a monolithic whole. Although many of them probably identify themselves as a collective entity with a common history and common culture – as West Indians – they still don't constitute an organic whole that is indivisible.

They also have their own differences in terms of how they see and perceive each other. For example, many Jamaicans, being from the biggest island in the Caribbean which they also arrogantly think is the best in every conceivable way, call other West Indians "small islanders"; not a term of endearment.

It is a derogatory term, although probably not as offensive as what some West Indians call Africans - "bush people,' "tree-climbing"creatures and other insults.

And it is virtually impossible to understand intergroup dynamics in these ethnic communities without first understanding that a very large number of people – if not the majority – in all these groups see themselves as having their own unique and separate identities different from those of other groups even if they are all linked by their common African heritage. After all, even in Africa itself, the Yoruba are not the same as the Zulu, or the Kikuyu the same as the Ewe in many fundamental respects. The list goes on and on.

Some of these observations - on relations between the members of these groups - are derived from my personal experience when I lived in Michigan in the United States and had the opportunity to interact with many African Americans and

Afro-Caribbeans on regular basis in the seventies and eighties; an opportunity I also had when I first arrived in the United States in 1972 and interacted with many African Americans in New York City and with a few Afro-Caribbeans in Washington, D.C. Some of these Afro-Caribbeans, from Trinidad, stayed with me when they visited Tanzania before I went to the United States. We were already in touch before they came to Tanzania.

I have also incorporated into my analysis the experiences of others in the United States and in the United Kingdom.

Although I have written about relations between Africans and African Americans in this book, the study of relations between continental Africans and the people of African descent in the diaspora cannot be complete and is not comprehensive enough without including Afro-Caribbeans and other Africans in the diaspora.

They are united yet divided, sometimes in a strange way, thus fuelling tensions among these groups. For example, a significant number of Africans and Afro-Caribbeans – not all but a significant number of them – are united in their stereotypical view of black Americans as a people who are not highly motivated and who don't take advantage of the abundant opportunities which exist for them to succeed in the land of opportunity, of milk and honey, this promised land of the United States.

And the fact that the members of these two groups on average have higher incomes than those of African Americans only reinforces the notion that black Americans are "lazy" or don't take life seriously and would rather spend their money on instant gratification than save for the future.

Coincidentally, it is a notion that was forcefully articulated by Professor Edward Banfield in his most influential and highly controversial book *The Unheavenly City: The Nature and Future f Our Urban Crisis* and other works and by other conservatives to justify government neglect of the poor, especially blacks and other minorities, in the United States.

He had profound impact on policy formulation when he acted as an adviser to Republican presidents and conservative law makers in Congress.

Banfield went on to argue that poverty, not racism, was the major problem black people face; ignoring the fact that racism itself is also responsible for much of the poverty black people face.

Many African and Afro-Caribbean immigrants subscribe to this highly offensive notion – that black Americans don't save their money but spend it right away for instant gratification - even if they are not necessarily ideological conservatives like Banfield and other rightwing scholars and ideologues.

But even higher levels of incomes especially among African immigrants should be looked at in their proper context. Intolerable conditions in Africa have forced many highly educated Africans to flee to the West. It is these conditions which explain why, for example, there are more than 30,000 Nigerian doctors in the United States; more than 600 Ghanaian doctors in New York City alone; and why in Chicago there are more doctors from Sierra Leone than there are in Sierra Leone.

Those are grim statistics. And they tell a sad story abut the conditions in our countries which force tens of thousands of highly educated people including professionals such as doctors, engineers, scientists and many others in different critical fields, to flee the continent every year in search of greener pastures in Western countries and elsewhere especially in the industrialized world.

But that is only the tip of the iceberg. Africa has suffered a massive brain drain through the years since independence in the sixties and continues to do so. And it is these immigrants who are at the centre of controversy between Africans and Afro-Caribbeans in Britain; and sometimes even between Africans and African Americans in the United States, although tensions between the two groups are not as highly pronounced or visibly expressed in many different ways including violent attacks as they are in the UK between African immigrants and black West Indians and their children.

Such high levels of achievement are, of course, a source of pride for many African immigrants and are even cited as a distinctive feature of their "unique" identity contrasted with that of Afro-Caribbeans and African Americans. And it feeds on itself, fuelling stereotypes about Afro-Caribbeans - especially in Britain - and about African Americans as non-achievers, unlike black African immigrants, thus exacerbating tensions which already exist between these groups.

Yet, when viewed from another perspective, the presence of a very large number of highly educated Africans in Britain and in the United States should be an embarrassment to Africans, and not something they should be proud of.

They are in America and in Britain and in other countries because their countries – in Africa – are messed up! Are they proud of the mess? They should be home helping their people and building their countries. Imagine if the 30,000 Nigerian doctors who live and work in the United States returned to Nigeria; and the doctors from Sierra Leone who live and work in Chicago alone returned to Sierra Leone. It would make a big difference in their countries.

Unfortunately, conditions in Africa don't allow or encourage these immigrants to go back home. They therefore remain in the West where they earn some of the highest incomes among all racial and ethnic groups because of their educational achievements across the spectrum. In fact, there are more Africans with Ph.D. degrees living and working in Western countries than they are in Africa.

Therefore their high incomes in the United States, Britain and elsewhere in the West - even of those with other degrees and not just doctorates - is directly proportional to their high levels of education, pushing the average income of African immigrants as a whole, or as groups, to a higher level than would have been the case had this push-pull factor not existed.

The majority of them would be in Africa if conditions back home were conducive to employment and the incomes of African immigrants who would have chosen to live and work in the West would have been lower than it is now.

The aggregate income of Africans in the West has been high for quite some now not only because of their high levels of education but also because of their professional experience; for example nurses who gained a lot of experience working in Nigeria, Kenya, Ghana, and Zimbabwe are now working in Britain.

This - high level of income among African immigrants as a group - was especially the case before the civil wars which forced many Africans including those with low education to seek refuge in the West. Many of the new immigrants fleeing from wars don't have much education like their brethren who willingly go to Western counties in pursuit of higher education or better job opportunities.

Yet there is no question that a very large number of Africans in Britain and in the United States, including students who are not immigrants, see themselves as high achievers. And this has inflated egos among many of them, making them think they are better than other people, especially African Americans – in the case of the United States – whom they don't see as achievers or hard workers; a stereotype which has also been used by white racists probably more than anybody else to belittle and dehumanize blacks since slavery.

It is a tragedy that a number of African and Afro-Caribbean immigrants harbour the same kind of stereotypes about black Americans; stereotypes which only serve a negative purpose of driving these groups farther and farther apart as if they have nothing in common.

So, in spite of the common history of suffering, and a common African heritage, tensions still exist between Africans and African Americans probably to an extent many people are not even aware of. As Michelle Boorstein, an Associated Press writer in New York, stated in her article on the subject, also posted on a Gambian discussion group on June 19, 2002:

> The poster on the wall at Louise's diner says, "Black is Black," but the people and the food here tell a more complicated story.
>
> Louise's sits in the heart of a neighborhood called Little Senegal, in central Harlem. Most of the faces you see along Little Senegal's wide boulevards and on the stoops of its brownstone homes are black - Africans and Americans both.
>
> As in any heavily immigrant neighborhood, culture here is a fusion: African-run restaurants offer dishes spiced gently for black Americans; groceries sell yam flakes and hamburgers; videos are available in English, French and the Senegalese language of Wolof.
>
> But members of the two communities say they live largely disconnected lives, praying, shopping and socializing among their own, sometimes harboring harsh stereotypes of one another.
>
> The separation is painful to many black Americans, who long for their lost historical roots. They rallied here in 1999 to protest the police killing of a West African immigrant, and they increasingly push for slavery reparations. They adopt Africa's hairstyles and adapt its music and wear T-shirts like one that

calls the faraway continent: "Home of the Original Black People."

"We're not as bonded as we should be," says Butch Williams, a 51-year-old steelworker, over a plate of eggs and grits at Louise's. The connection to Africa is "one of THE ongoing questions for black Americans," he says. "You look around and you say, 'What tribe am I from?' You can't help but wonder."

The disconnect has no such meaning to many African immigrants, who often come to this country to make money and then return home. They don't necessarily see life in America as black vs. white. "You go on with your life and them with theirs," says Adam Fofana, who came here from the Ivory Coast eight years ago and runs a restaurant called Fatou - down the street from Louise's.

Still, Fatou offers food that Fofana hopes will bring all blacks in Little Senegal together: West African and Caribbean fare and an all-American beer, Budweiser. So far, the clientele is strictly West African.

Talk about the intergroup dynamics has grown in the past decade with the dramatic swell of African immigrants to New York City neighborhoods, including Harlem. (The number of immigrants to New York from Ghana alone increased 220 percent from the mid to late 1990s; from Nigeria, 380 percent. Figures for all nationalities are not available.)

A new French film called "Little Senegal" is about a Senegalese man who comes to Harlem and the profound rift he finds there.

And in the next few months, museums in New York and Philadelphia will hold programs exploring the topic. "Africans want to make money (in the United States) and go home. African-Americans want them to play their citizenship role and have solidarity as black people. They have two different agendas," said Manthia Diawara, a Malian filmmaker who heads the Africana Studies Department at New York University and has written extensively about black culture.

The divide was highlighted for the world two years ago when four white New York City police officers shot Amadou Diallo, an unarmed immigrant from Guinea, 41 times.

Black Americans took to the streets to protest what they saw as a racist attack and were shocked to find their fervor largely unmatched by their African neighbors.

Yet Africans who immigrate here say they don't necessarily feel closer to black Americans than to anyone else. In fact, they often have their own set of negative stereotypes. "My father told me not to be friends with black people in America," said Cheick Sissoko, a 27-year-old dancer and drummer who came from Ivory Coast five years ago and now lives in lower Manhattan. "What we see on TV is so bad - guns and everything. Then I come and I realize it's true."

Fofana, the restaurant owner, says black Americans think they're above the sort of gritty work immigrants must do to establish themselves in a new country. For black Americans who ache from that lost connection, such sentiments can sting.

At Djoniba, the downtown Manhattan dance center where Sissoko works, dancers of all colors and backgrounds take classes ranging from the style of the Mandingo tribe in West Africa to Congolese, Haitian and hip-hop. The only actual Africans there are the teachers, but students wearing traditional African fabrics and others in Lycra bicycle unitards mingle alongside posters advertising vacations in Africa. "Come home!" one says.

Some of the black American dancers say they resent that the African teachers don't feel a special connection to them, don't recognize that there is a reason they are doing African dance rather than kickboxing or Roller-blading.

"There's not a sense of cultural solidarity between African-Americans and Africans, and we are always looking for that connection," said Tracy Austin, a 45-year-old black corporate lawyer who lives in Harlem and has been involved with the Senegalese community here for many years. "I think a lot of African-Americans are responding to that lack of solidarity, that sense that there is a lack of race-consciousness among Africans, which we have very deeply."

According to John Arthur, a University of Minnesota sociologist and anthropologist and Ghana native who has researched African migration to the United States, part of the reason for the gap is that a key stretch of the bridge is missing. The slave trade is not a regular part of the curriculum in many schools in Africa, and Arthur believes that this is because Africans would prefer not to face their role in the industry. As a result, he says, "they don't understand that they do have a connection."

While it is common for immigrants in general to insist that they will return to their native country, it is more so among Africans, says Arthur, author of a book on the subject called *Invisible Sojourners*.

Mabel Haddock, head of a Harlem-based group that promotes films about blacks, says black Americans' longing for Africa is like other romanticized feelings people have for places. Many African films, she says, explore the longing of people for their hometowns after they migrate to large cities. "I think some people have this rather exotic vision of what Africa is," said Haddock, head of the National Black Programming Consortium, "that if you go there you'll find something better than here that's better for your spiritual self."

Waly Ndiaye, a 49-year-old translator from Senegal who lives in Little Senegal, says he thinks black Americans who focus on their history in Africa and on slavery should think about the future. "I think people need to forget and move on. No matter how hard it was, there are a lot of opportunities," he said.

But in a reminder of the depth of the connection, Ndiaye adds that he and his African friends can tell what part of the continent black Americans were originally from by their look - and their smell.

Ndiaye said he was brought to tears by "Little Senegal." The film tells the story of Alloune, a widower who runs tours at Goree Island, once a slave export center off the coast of West Africa. Upon retirement, he travels to the United States in search of his ancestors who were brought here as slaves.

Among its characters: a fat, money-obsessed black American who refers to an African mechanic as "a big ape"; an African immigrant who whips his girlfriend, a pregnant African-American teenager, and an African who says "we're too black" for black Americans.

Depending on one's viewpoint, "Little Senegal" is jammed with simplistic caricatures - or truths. To some, the film's African characters are idealized - wise, educated, family-oriented and proud, while its black Americans are rootless, materialistic, crude about topics like sex and love and cold about topics like parenting and community.

Others say it was evenhanded and note that an African character loathed American blacks even while admitting he had taken no interest in getting to know them - an insular attitude black Americans in Little Senegal say is dead-on.

What exactly prompted Ndiaye's tears shows how complex the issue is. He was moved both by the notion of an African coming to America to find his roots - that the two communities DO share roots - and by the fact that Alloune did not try to bring the Americans he met back to Africa, home to Africa.

For now, the relationship remains part history and part myth, distant and close.

While Fofana hangs drawings of slain American black nationalist leader Malcolm X on the walls of Fatou, a map of Africa is up at Louise's.

"Simply because our skins are black doesn't mean we have anything in common," said Williams, the steelworker eating breakfast. "But we do."

The disdain and contempt for black Americans among some Africans and black West Indians, as well as the indifference towards them, assumes another dimension when they unfairly compare their fate – as a people from independent countries - with that of African Americans who have been perpetually condemned to a minority status in a predominantly white society which has never accepted them as equal human beings.

Some of them think they are better than black Americans because they come from black independent countries such as Nigeria, Kenya, Ghana and Tanzania, while American blacks don't have a country of their own, ignoring the fact that it's not their fault.

James Baldwin articulated a collective sentiment in his book *The Fire Next Time* in which he recalled a conversation he had with Elijah Muhammad and other members of the black Nation of Islam in Chicago in the early sixties. And it captured the essence of the suffering, humiliation and frustration black Americans have to endure all their lives as a powerless minority in a white racist society.

Such powerlessness is also a brutal reminder that their ancestors were sold into slavery by the ancestors of some of the very same people who despise them so much; and who are even related to them since they are all children of Africa, only separated by slavery.

However, it should also be emphasized that it is probably only a minority – at least those openly hostile - who harbour such notions of superiority over black Americans. It is highly unlikely that the majority of Africans and Afro-Caribbeans look down upon black Americans simply because they don't have a country of their own or because of some other reason or reasons.

Yet the "homelessness" of African Americans has also been seized upon by many black nationalists, including militants, in the United States as a rallying cry to mobilize blacks in their quest for an independent homeland for the descendants of African slaves "trapped" in the land of their birth.

Prominent among them are the Black Muslims and members of the Republic of New Afrika all of whom have demanded five to six southern states to establish an independent black nation; a far cry from reality, yet understandable, borne out of desperation.

In his conversation with Elijah Muhammad and a number of other Black Muslims, James Baldwin said he was struck by Elijah Muhammad's comment that no people in history had ever been respected who had not owned their own land; to which others at the table responded, "Yes, that's right." And as Baldwin stated in *The Fire Next Time*:

> I could not deny the truth of this statement. For everyone else has, is, a nation, with a specific location, and a flag – even, these days, the Jew. It is only 'the so-called American Negro' who remains trapped, disinherited, and despised, in a nation that has kept him in bondage for nearly four hundred years and is still unable to recognize him as a human being. - (James Baldwin, *The Fire Next Time*, New York, 1964, pp. 100 – 101).

Yet in spite of the shared disdain and contempt for black Americans common among some Africans and Afro-Caribbeans, this strange bond of unity between them is not strong enough to keep them united against black Americans.

All three groups are some times united as one. They are also united with one or the other against one of them. And they are all against each other for different reasons under different circumstances.

Thus, you have many black Americans and black West Indians who are united in their contempt for Africans and in their belief that Africa is a primitive, backward continent full of savages and ignorant people dying of hunger and disease, incapable of learning and helping themselves, and dependent on international relief for survival; with educated Africans themselves in the United States and elsewhere – even in Africa itself – hardly removed from such primitive conditions and even bringing all kinds of diseases and habits of poor hygiene with them to the United States and other parts of the civilized world especially the West.

Then you have a number of Africans and African Americans sharing a common belief that people from the islands, especially Jamaicans, are notorious for using and selling drugs. We hear about Jamaican criminal gangs and the Jamaican Mafia wreaking havoc in different communities in the United States. But there is an African counterpart: Nigerian criminal gangs and the Nigerian Mafia, as well as the 419 Nigerian scam we hear so much about. Yet, in both cases, the criminal elements don't constitute the largest number of people in those groups.

And there is another complaint against Afro-Caribbeans, many of whom call themselves and would rather be called West Indians and not Afro-Caribbeans.

Some Africans and African Americans complain that black people from the Caribbean think that they are better than Africans and black Americans and don't even want to be called or call themselves black – lest they be lumped together with black Americans in the ghetto and elsewhere, and with primitive Africans, as the the same people.

I personally have heard some prejudiced and ignorant Jamaicans say they have nothing to do with Africa and did not come from Africa; a sentiment shared by some prejudiced and ignorant black Americans as well. Yet, it is a minority view in both cases.

I also remember one Zimbabwean in Britain saying he knew some Jamaicans who said they "hate Africans" and "can't stand Africans"; again a minority view among the vast majority of Afro-Caribbeans in the UK.

However, it has ripple effect and shows that there are tensions in relations between Africans and black West Indians, also between Africans and African Americans, and between West Indians and African Americans.

I have also heard some Jamaicans and Trinidadians using derogatory remarks to describe black Americans not only as "lazy" but also as "morally depraved," "promiscuous" and having babies out of wedlock while living on welfare at the expense of hardworking people such as themselves – black West Indians or Afro-Caribbeans – who take care of them with their taxes; deliberately ignoring the fact that most black Americans work and don't live on welfare.

Many Africans also have the same low opinion of African Americans. They also say many black Americans don't go school or simply drop out of school even when they have scholarships; and that they come from broken homes, can't be trusted, and steal a lot, breaking and entering, robbing people, petrol (gas) stations, banks and other businesses. The list goes on and on.

Black West Indians, of course, also have the same stereotypes about American blacks, in spite of empirical evidence showing that only a very small number of black Americans commit crime.

Yet, whether or not such sentiments are a product of ignorance or are deliberately intended to be insults, there is no question that none of this has helped to facilitate constructive dialogue between Africans and Afro-Caribbeans or between African Americans and Afro-Caribbeans; nor has it helped improve relations between Africans and African Americans which have been described by some observers as "strained" and even "bad."

In the United Kingdom, there have been reports about rising tensions between Africans and Afro-Caribbeans. For example in May 2006, the BBC's "Politics Show" focused on tensions between black West Indians and Africans in London. And as one Afro-Caribbean, Joseph Collins from Guyana, stated on BBC Africa, 15 August 2003:

> I have found that Africans who come from countries with deep ethnic cleavages are less tolerant of other blacks. For example look at the Nigerian-Jamaican tensions in London.
> The fact that Jamaicans and other West Indians have black skins doesn't mean a thing to the average Nigerian.
> Pan-Africanism is dead. More than ever before. Continental Africans are tuned in to bio-cultural signifiers such as accent and skin-colour.

All these tensions are in addition to what is already happening among different racial groups which clash now and then in different parts of Britain.

In 2004, The London *Guardian* had an article on this very

same subject in which the writer, Darcus Howe, who was also a broadcaster, stated that after 50 years of racist attacks on immigrants, conflict between West Indians, Asians and Africans was increasing. His documentary "Who You Callin' a Nigger" was also broadcast on television in the UK. As he stated in his article, "Turning on Each Other," in *The Guardian*, August 7, 2004:

> Anti-immigrant racism has, for close to 50 years, offered perks to those at the top of the racial hierarchy here in Britain. Jobs, promotion once at work, access to careers which are almost exclusively open to those with white skins are but some of them.
>
> It is inevitable that among immigrants and their offspring, copycat divisions would appear. We have supped from the cup. And just as that wider conflict expresses itself in violent racial attacks, so will the phenomenon repeat itself among Asians and West Indians.
>
> This antisocial activity has raised its ugly head in jets of violence, if hardly on the scale of white racism. It is certainly not as deep-rooted; nevertheless, it exists, and if allowed to continue can transform areas of the inner city into very nasty places.
>
> I celebrate my 21st anniversary in broadcasting with a documentary titled, "Who You Callin' a Nigger." It reports on violent confrontations between West Indians and Somalis in South London and between West Indian and Pakistani youths in the Midlands.
>
> There are comments from Asian men and women which are wholly disparaging of their fellow migrants from the Caribbean, and equally vitriolic language from West Indians about Somalis.
>
> It was very difficult listening to all this throughout the filming and in the editing studio. There have been frail deposits of this phenomenon as far back as I can remember, but it never went beyond banter between West Indians and Africans, totally devoid of any rationale that attempted to justify it.
>
> It was merely a dissonance that occurs when strangers meet without prior introduction. It is only in recent times that these deposits have matured into full blown violence, as has happened between West Indian and Somali youths in Plumstead and Woolwich.
>
> My activism in the black community over the last 40 years included fierce and unrelenting campaigns on issues of the final liberation of Africans from colonialism. Mrs Howe actually held the platform with Amilcar Cabral at a hot meeting organised in support of Africans against Portuguese colonialism. Then there was the anti-apartheid movement and the birth of Zimbabwe.
>
> Then, an entire generation of West Indians in the UK could be relied on to stand tall.
>
> Not, it seems, now. I journeyed through Woolwich and Plumstead, where thousands of Somali refugees are settling. The Caribbean community is mostly unwelcoming. Some visit on Somalis the same kind of racial abuse we suffered in the period of early migration. Dissenters to this reactionary view are few and

far between. "They are taking our houses. They are getting social benefits which are denied to us. Their children are overcrowding our schools." And more.

One middle-aged West Indian woman capped her experiences at the hand of a group of young Somalis with uninhibited outburst: "I hate Somalis. They should go back to where they came from." She did not bat an eyelid.

Parts of Woolwich and Plumstead can only be described as the pits. The surrounding docklands offer no economic activity. Some housing stock depresses even optimists among social activists. Both communities of dark skin forage for a handful of employment opportunities. White Greenwich, a spit away, thrives, while citizens of Plumstead and parts of Woolwich can only feel teased and taunted by their neighbours' success.

The Somalis are a captive community in the grip of self-appointed community leaders. One of them slapped around the documentary director because we did not ask his permission to film his subjects.

And off to Walsall, just outside Birmingham. I had not visited there for close to 25 years when waves of West Indians and Asians (in particular Pakistanis) converged at first shift to set in motion the engineering factories which served the motor industry. The wages from this mass industrial activity supported whole communities.

It's all gone now, leaving a wasteland, and new generations of Pakistanis and West Indian youths at each other throats with little social activity to mediate the conflict.

The virus which produces this conflict has also infected small Asian businessmen and the clerical lower middle classes who inhabit nearby Handsworth. The small Asian entrepreneur is slowly losing its captive clientele to large supermarkets and department stores. And there is a mad scramble for clerical jobs in the civil service, local councils and banks.

I spent some time with a Punjabi small businessman. He sells Indian sweets and a young generation of Punjabis ignores his wares for Mars bars, jelly babies, Bounty bars and the rest. He sees enemies everywhere. His primary target is the West Indian community, then the Russians and east Europeans. He belches forth the most lurid abuse he can muster.

My difficulties did not end with the filming and editing. I anticipate a return of hurdles I have long transcended in my earlier work at Channel 4. The first is positive images. My detractors will charge that such a documentary will strengthen the cause of the BNP. As I see it, our Asian businessman is already classic BNP material and I reply to those who make the charge only that the programme represents the truth.

Dirty linen needs airing. We have to be mercilessly realistic to make any assessment of who and where we are.

It is impossible for a section of the immigrant community to avoid gravitating to racial categorisation when the practice is so rewarding for the indigenous population. This challenges us all: we face it, we die or we run away.

The phenomenon is not unique to London. In other parts of the

Britain, many members of different immigrants groups are hostile or indifferent towards. And they sometimes clash even if physical confrontations are not the main feature of their tempestuous relationships as neighbours or simply as fellow countrymen. It equally applies to black immigrant groups in spite of their common African heritage.

Afro-Caribbeans and Africans have had a stormy relationship sometimes erupting in violence even if it has been downplayed by some leaders and community activists on both sides, especially those of the Pan-Africanist kind who would rather "ignore" such clashes and tensions for the sake of racial solidarity.

The tensions are ignited and fuelled by a combination of factors including competition for jobs, housing and social services. Many Afro-Caribbeans in Britain also feel that, because they have been in the UK longer than a disproportionately large of African immigrants especially newer arrivals, they are entitled to a privileged status and should be the first in line to get jobs, housing and social services.

The tensions between the two groups are also exacerbated by stereotypes about each other, even by stereotypes which correspond to reality; for example the high incidence of crime among Afro-Caribbean youths many of whom also use and sell drugs and are also involved in gang warfare with Asian gangs – Indian and Pakistani – a phenomenon not so common in the African immigrant community in the UK.

Violent crime is also on the rise among Afro-Caribbean youths using guns, although the use of such weapons is not exclusive to the Afro-Caribbean community.

And many victims of this wave of crime by West Indians are Africans some of whom have even been killed, further alienating the African community in the UK. As Dr. Perry Stanislas, an Afro-Caribbean and senior lecturer at Leicester de Montfort University in Britain, stated in an interview with *Black Britain* in November 2006, in terms of violent crime especially robbery, drug-related crime and gun crime, "We are talking essentially about African Caribbeans," an assessment based on empirical evidence.

He went on to say that the offending rate of continental Africans is not as significant as that of African Caribbeans, but there is a pattern of Africans being involved in particular types of crimes, fraud being the most obvious. As he put it: "Fraud has a long history with West Africans going back to the 1950s."

Established West African communities, especially of Nigerians and Ghanaians, have a long history in Britain. The communities were largely formed by Ghanaians and Nigerians who arrived in the UK after World War II.

And in terms of historical experience, they are different from newer immigrant groups of Africans. Yet they face discrimination in a way West Indians don't, in spite of their high levels of education.

Dr. Stanislas went on to say in the same interview with *Black Britain* that a sad reality for the West African community in Britain is "the massive disparity between educational qualifications and the type of jobs that they do."

He explained that this is because the pattern of discrimination against West Africans is far more intense than that experienced by African Caribbeans.

The reason for the increased discrimination against Africans generally is because they are still perceived as outsiders because they have retained more of their culture than Afro-Caribbeans have, particularly in terms of language and cultural values and African names, which is perceived as a threat to those who would prefer immigrants to be more integrated and assimilated and look, sound and dress like "British people"; in many cases a euphemism for white Britons except in the case of looks since black West Indians will *never* look white even if some of them delude themselves into believing that they are indeed "white"!

Dr. Stanislas further stated: "There is greater suspicion towards them." This is despite the fact that significant numbers of West Africans were actually born in Britain. "It does not help where you have a perception of dishonesty in terms of fraud and identification fraud against particular communities."

Over the last ten years, roughly since the mid-nineties, there has been unprecedented media coverage of fraud involving West Africans, whilst white-collar crime committed by middle-class whites and others is not investigated or reported except for major cases like that of Enron and which are still the exception rather than the rule in terms of investigation and exposure.

Such bias was demonstrated when the BBC ran a headline on 20 November 2006 saying "Nigeria scams 'cost UK billions'" in a story which reported that financial crime in the UK originating from Nigeria costs the UK economy £150m a year, according to a study by Chatham House.

Dr Stanislas told *Black Britain* that whilst it may be a minority involved in such scams, the whole West African community is perceived in negative terms and labelled as being dishonest.

He also uncovered during his research a court case around 10 years ago in which a black West Indian judge, Leonard Woodley, said increasingly large numbers of West Africans, Nigerians in particular, seem to be coming to the UK for only one reason, which is fraud.

It was a biased statement coming from the bench, reinforcing stereotypes about Africans and did not help foster good relations between Africans and members of the black West Indian community who already have their own negative stereotypes about Africans and the African continent itself.

The perception of Africans as being dishonest and that there is massive involvement among West African communities in fraudulent crime does in itself lead to greater discrimination when it comes to employment, provision of services and in other areas including housing.

Both whites and West Indians – as well as other people – engage in such discrimination against West Africans and other African immigrants, although in varying degrees.

But it is focused and sometimes intense. And as Dr. Stanislas noted further: "What we are (also) sure of is that the West African community suffer more intensely from discrimination and that they earn less than African Caribbeans"; which may be a contributory factor to some of their involvement in crime.

He said that there may be some people in the West African community - as well as in other African immigrant groups - who are well-established in Britain who may become frustrated by the lack of opportunities.

Recent arrivals such as Somalis have similar experiences with frustration and may gravitate towards crime as a means of livelihood.

Yet, in spite of all these problems, Africans commit less crime than West Indians do; and save money more than Afro-Caribbeans do, although they earn less and not commensurate with their educational qualifications and experience.

Dr Stanislas said that older sections of the West African community are under far more pressure from discrimination than their brethren are. He also said compared with Africans, there are fewer Afro-Caribbeans who maintain two jobs. And although both Africans and Afro-Caribbeans send money home, this is more prevalent among Africans.

According to the Department for International Development's BME Remittance Survey in July 2006, 34 per cent of Africans send money home, compared with 12 per cent of African Caribbeans. The same survey revealed that Ghana derives 10 -15 per cent of its national income from such remittances, compared to just 3 per cent from foreign investment.

The strong work ethic among Africans in Britain, as elsewhere where they have established immigrant communities, is clearly evident even to a casual observer in spite of stereotypes of "lazy" Africans.

There is evidence showing that Africans are more likely to have families to support on the continent and many maintain two to three jobs to make ends meet in a society which discriminates against them in the job market resulting in a lower income than that of other immigrants who are less qualified. As Dr. Stanislas stated: "There is a lot of pressure [and] under these circumstances it is not unreasonable to assume that a small number will look for unorthodox means in order to increase their income."

Africans are also victimized in other ways black West Indians are not, setting the groups further apart, in spite of the fact that immigrants in the African community are no worse than Afro-Caribbeans or other Britons in terms of morality and personal values. They are just human beings. Yet, they are not always treated as equals by many black West Indians and by the majority of whites and people of other races.

One of the areas in which they are victimized in highly disproportionate numbers is crime. As Dr. Stanislas put it: "Africans are more likely to be exposed to crime by the mere fact that they are more concentrated in the most run-down crime-ridden estates."

He went on to say one of the reasons "Africans are more likely to be victims of crime" is that there is less private ownership amongst them compared with Afro-Caribbeans.

And regardless of qualifications Africans, earn less than Afro-Caribbeans do for no other reason than that they are seen as outsiders, besides racism which also affects black West Indians; and more of them live on run-down council estates which are a breeding ground for crime "and high levels of victimisation," as Dr Stanislas put it.

He cited the case of 40 year-old Steven NyemboYa Muteb, a university student and father of two from Congo, who was stabbed to death by black West Indians in 2006 after complaining of anti-social behaviour by them on the Hackney council estate where he lived.

Ten-year-old Nigerian-born Damilola Taylor was another victim, also murdered by black West Indian youths on a Peckham housing estate in November 2000.

According to Dr. Stanislas: "What I am suggesting is that it could well be that Africans are more likely to be exposed to crime by the mere fact that they are more concentrated in the most run-down crime-ridden estates," and also which have large numbers of Afro-Caribbean immigrants; a significant number of whom don't identify themselves with African immigrants just as many continental Africans don't identify with them.

And as reported by *The Guardian*, London, 3 October 2006, the residents where the Congolese lived had also - like the Congolese who was murdered - complained about antisocial behaviour at the estate. According to the report, "Father Killed After Tackling Gang of Youths":

A churchgoing father of two was stabbed to death in the stairwell of his block of flats after confronting a gang of youths and asking them to be quiet because he was trying to sleep.

Steven Nyembo-Ya-Muteb, 40, tackled the group of up to 12 youngsters late on Sunday evening after they broke into the communal entrance of the flats on a council estate in Hackney, east London. Police said he managed to force most of the youths to leave but two returned, pulling a knife on the mature student.

It is understood that a neighbour found Mr Nyembo-Ya-Muteb bleeding to death on the stairwell. He was pronounced dead at nearby Homerton hospital.

Simon Pountain, police borough commander for Hackney, said the dead man acted reasonably. "He did what any normal citizen should do. It just happens that one or more of the youths were such that they decided to go back and attack him."

He warned members of the public against putting themselves in danger when confronting gangs but said Mr Nyembo-Ya-Muteb had done nothing wrong. "We should all be able to challenge young people. But those who do that must take account of the risks involved."

Jennette Arnold, London assembly member for the area, said: "At a time when people prefer to say nothing Mr Nyembo-Ya-Muteb spoke out. We owe him a debt. He was a decent citizen."

Mr Pountain said the father of two girls, five and six, was alone in the flat when he challenged the gang. "They came into the communal area and were creating the disturbance. After Steven successfully ushered them out, that was when one or more came back into the foyer, the communal area, and attacked him."

Four youths have been arrested, including a 15-year-old and a 17-year-old.

Mr Nyembo-Ya-Muteb, from Congo, was in his third year of studying maths at university and regularly attended Edmonton Methodist church.

Neighbours said the youths were smoking cannabis and probably gained access to the building by climbing through an unlocked first floor window.

Forensics officers spent the morning dusting and collecting fingerprints. The window is below a CCTV camera and it is understood that the forced entry may have been recorded.

One woman who lives in the building said that it was plagued with problems and that less than three months ago the entrance had to be fitted with a metal door in an attempt to stop drug users and prostitutes coming into the stairwell.

Another neighbour, Steven Morris, said: "It's just a constant trouble. Every night we have it. There's prostitutes, smackheads, people having sex on the stairs."

Jeanette Hockley, 72, who lives in the building, said Mr Nyembo-Ya-Muteb moved in four years ago with his wife and daughters. "He was a very nice man, very sociable and friendly."

A noticeboard opposite the block of flats where Mr Nyembo-Ya-Muteb lived reflects the extent to which the area was troubled by antisocial behaviour. A police message says: "After successful operations in this area a large number of arrests have been made for drug dealing. The residents are actively working with us to identify those responsible. It will not be long before your identities are known and action taken against you."

Eric Ollerenshaw, Hackney council's opposition leader, said residents had complained about antisocial behaviour. "The police promised to increase patrols and that did happen for a while but this will set everything back again. Community support officers work 9am until 5pm but the yobs are there around the clock."

The killing will heighten anxiety about the risks of confronting antisocial behaviour.

Peter Woodhams was shot in Custom House, east London, in August after he confronted a gang of youths causing trouble outside his home. Mr Woodhams's funeral took place yesterday.

Not all West Indians commit crime; in fact most of them don't. And most of them don't have a negative attitude towards Africans and vice versa. But a large number of them do, and in terms of crime, a much higher percentage of the crime perpetrated in the Black British community – which includes Afro-Caribbeans and Africans – is committed by West Indians, accentuating cleavages between the two groups.

Black-on-black crime is a major problem in the black community in the UK just as it is in the black community in the United States.

West Indians, especially Jamaicans, also have a reputation as drug couriers smuggling drugs into Britain and even into the United States and Canada.

Some Africans especially Nigerians and Ghanaians do, of course, have the same reputation as drug couriers although it is believed - and there is statistical evidence showing - that Jamaicans and other West Indians smuggle more drugs into the UK and at a much higher rate than Africans do. And as Professor Ben Bowling, Britain's leading black criminologist and director of criminological studies at King's College School of Law in London stated in an interview with *Black Britain* in October 2006:

> The organised crime groups are using typically poor, rural West Indians as drugs couriers.
> The illegal drugs market creates huge opportunities for organised crime groups to pay modest amounts of money to move the drugs around.

African immigrants in Britain also cite other evidence which shows that they are different from and better off than black West Indians.

They have strong families – as much as they do a strong work ethic - at a much higher percentage than Afro-Caribbeans do, best exemplified by two-parent homes unlike many families in the West Indian community which are matrifocal and surviving on welfare more than the families of African immigrants are.

It is also one of the factors that also partly explains the higher incidence of crime in the West Indian community.

The absence of a father or a father figure at home contributes to deterioration of the home environment. Lack of discipline among many West Indian youths is one of the biggest causes of crime in the black community – and poor performance in school at a higher rate among West Indians - which also affects many African immigrants living in the same areas together with black West Indians. And it shapes attitudes of Africans towards West Indians.

And as high achievers in school, and in employment because of their high levels of education among other things, many African immigrants don't see themselves as being on the same level with the vast majority of Afro-Caribbeans whom they have surpassed in many areas of education.

Motivation is also one of the factors African immigrants cite to explain their success in life as immigrants in Britain; an attribute shared by their brethren in other West countries where they have settled in large numbers.

Therefore many of the stereotypes about black West Indians are also reinforced by empirical evidence, and studies, showing that many African immigrants in the United Kingdom – and even in the United States – have higher incomes and education than Afro-Caribbeans and African Americans, respectively; although in the United Kingdom, many Africans at all levels of education don't earn as much as black West Indians because of discrimination. As an anglicized community, black West Indians – stripped of their African culture and identity – are seen as more British and are more accepted by white Britons than Africans are.

Such disparity and discrimination also fuels tensions between Africans and West Indians in the UK.

And the motivation factor, inextricably linked with family background in most cases, is critical to success among all groups regardless of race or ethnicity. As Douglas Muganhiri, a black African in Zimbabwe, stated in his comment on 22 Mach 2002 on a special report on the BBC, "Are Black Pupils Getting A Raw Deal?" because of their under-performance in school in Britain:

> I feel the black children can still do better even if the system disadvantages them, that is if their black parents are willing.
> I come from a Black country (Zimbabwe), where children do very well in school despite the lack of many basic school requirements.

The problem, I think, with black children overseas is that they lack proper orientation and encouragement particularly from their parents.

Kids need to be made aware of the advantages of excelling at school at a very early stage in life in order for them to appreciate why one must attend lessons at school, why one must be well behaved at school. Telling children that learning is a white domain doesn't help black kids at all.

We are a poor black country here, but we have one of the world's most highly educated populations, despite the economic problems, because our parents made us think that school is good.

So, overseas black kids, you are lucky you have everything at school plus free education. Here we go to school hungry, with not enough equipment and education is NOT free, but we still pass at school.

Intelligence knows no colour.

Another black African named Tiseke from Malawi, who was also studying in the UK during that time, had this to say on the same subject and on the differences between black Africans and Afro-Caribbeans in Britain in terms of achievement in school and, by implication, in life in general:

Please stop lumping Afro-Caribbeans with Africans just because we are all black.

I was educated in Africa and one thing that I can tell you is that despite the terrible poverty and political upheaval on our continent Africans work very hard in school when they can afford to attend them and this is despite the many obstacles they face in their day to day lives.

I studied for my Masters degree in the Netherlands and those of us who were Africans did much better than the white Dutch and those from Suriname.

I am now doing my PhD in the UK and I see the same thing. The Africans work much harder at educating themselves.

Maybe the problem over here is that you (white and black African/Caribbean but born in Britain) know that you are still going to get benefit/welfare even if you don't succeed in school a luxury that those of us in Africa do not have!

The vast majority of African immigrants, most of them from poverty-stricken countries, take those values and attitudes with them when they emigrate from Africa and settle in other countries including Britain. And that accounts for their success in many areas in life in their adopted countries.

Unfortunately, instead of being a source of inspiration, the success of a disproportionately large number of black African immigrants in the UK is one of the main factors fuelling tensions between the members of these two immigrant groups and their children born and brought up in Britain. For example, Nigerians in the black community in the UK have a reputation for studying hard and ding very well in school; so do other Africans, of course, but Nigerians stand out because of their relatively large number in the African immigrant community.

Yet it is also a fact that they have demonstrated success, as clearly shown by the large number of very highly educated Nigerians in many fields in the UK and elsewhere including the United States.

West Indian immigrants are more frustrated than inspired by the success of African immigrants. And they feel victimized when Africans get jobs they can't get, or housing they can't get, but to which they feel they are more entitled than African immigrants are because they were there first, as earlier immigrants.

There is another factor that should not be overlooked as a driving force towards success among many African immigrants both in the UK and in the United States – as well as in other countries, of course. Poverty has served as a very powerful motivating factor among many Africans, especially those who don't have much education.

A very large number of them come from very poor families. They had very little where they came from. So when they arrive in Britain or in the United States, they see opportunities everywhere even where such opportunities don't even exist! But because even delusions or myths – of abundant opportunities and wealth – can serve as an incentive. Many of these immigrants create opportunities for themselves, using whatever skills they have, and doing whatever they can, and taking whatever jobs they can get, however low-paying, to make it in life.

And some of them do succeed in life, climbing up the social and economic ladder. And when they succeed after working so hard, they automatically conclude that opportunities exist for anybody to succeed in life and people who don't succeed – many Afro-Caribbeans and African Americans in this case – simply don't want to work or take advantage of the opportunities that are available to them to make it in life just like everybody else does. They take jobs African Americans – or long-term immigrants such as West Indians or Afro-Caribbeans - don't want to take for different reasons including low wages; and they see opportunities where African Americans and Afro-Caribbeans don't see any.

One of the main reasons people like West Indians and African Americans born and brought up in Britain and in the United States don't see those opportunities is that they are used to a higher standard of living the new immigrants are not used to. And what is opportunity for the newly arrived immigrants is not opportunity for them – and they would rather go on welfare, at least some of them, than work for very low wages or take jobs they consider to be demeaning or beneath them.

All this fuels stereotypes on both sides. The native-born make fun of immigrants saying they take anything or accept anything! And the immigrants say these people are just lazy, don't want to work, and think they are better than others.

The result is strained relations between the immigrants and the native-born, sometimes leading to confrontations in varying degrees even if not necessarily in a violent way. But there have been some violent confrontations, especially between Africans and Afro-Caribbeans, although the vast majority on both sides neither condone nor support that.

However, even verbal exchanges can get downright nasty regardless of the economic and social status of those involved. Many middle-class Africans and West Indians involved in these exchanges are just as much capable of using coarse language. As British Professor Christie Davies stated in *The Social Affairs Unit*, 22 December 2006:

> When there is a dispute between British Nigerians and British Jamaicans and it gets to exchange of abuse time, middle-class Nigerians will reach for the word "slave!", as in "I don't take that kind of talk from a slave", because they know it will enrage the Jamaicans more than any other epithet.

There have also been clashes between Asians and Afro-Caribbeans as well as Africans in the UK. Asians see Africans and Afro-Caribbeans simply as one people because they are all black, even though many people in those groups don't necessarily feel that way. They see themselves as different ethnic groups, each with its own unique identity and history.

The worst tensions in Britain are between Asians and Afro-Caribbeans, besides white racist groups. Tensions between Afro-Caribbean residents and Asians in a number of regions in Britain have led to confrontations, including the violent disturbances in Birmingham in 2005 where groups from both communities fought and rioted over two nights.

There is also evidence not only of tensions, but of rising tensions, between the members of the Afro-Caribbean community and the growing number of African immigrants at a time when anti-foreign sentiments in Britain are also gaining ground, thus making things worse for both groups in a predominantly white society where many whites simply tolerate them.

What is so disturbing is that in spite of noble intentions by some individuals in both groups – African and Afro-Caribbean – to defuse tensions, a significant number of people on both sides still don't see themselves as one people and are determined to maintain their separate identities as "Africans" and as "West Indians" - the latter being a preferable term to some of those who don't want to be called "Afro-Caribbeans," a distinctive appellation that automatically identifies them with "primitive" Africa and Africans.

Yet, there are many black West Indians or Afro-Caribbeans who identify with Africa and are not ashamed of their heritage deeply rooted in this maligned continent, the "darkest" of all continents where even light cannot escape as if it were a black hole, as some pundits would have us believe!

And I'm not talking about just those who are politically conscious, for example people like Professor Horace Campbell from Jamaica and Dr. Walter Rodney from Guyana who taught at the University of Dar es Salaam in my home country, Tanzania. I'm talking about ordinary Afro-Caribbeans some of whom have been met with hostility from Africans even when they make genuine attempts to identify with Africa and Africans.

One particular incident comes to mind in this case.

When I was a student at Wayne State University in Detroit in the state of Michigan in the United States in the mid-seventies, there was a Jamaican medical student who wanted to interact with Africans a lot of times. And a lot of times there were some Africans, although only a few, who were openly hostile towards him and told him he was not an African and did not even want him to play soccer with them.

Yet, these were some of the "enlightened" Africans, college

students, who had seen the light. Still, they could not see beyond the curtain of prejudice which blinded them to reality as much as it did those in the diaspora who hated Africa and Africans with equal passion and intensity in spite of their African heritage which would remain an integral part of their identity although they were not born and brought up in Africa but were descended from African slaves forcibly uprooted from their motherland and transported to the Americas in chains.

More than 30 years later, I can still hear the echo of his voice, from that Jamaican student, telling his tormentors, "I am an African like you."

His harshest critic was a Nigerian engineering student who remained adamant in his position saying, "You are not an African. You are not one of us." And I knew both well.

Fortunately, the Jamaican student was accepted by the majority of the African students he interacted with, and they refused to ostracize him.

Other Afro-Caribbeans who are known for their identification with Africa include the Rastafarians, although their identification with Ethiopia almost exclusively – where they did not originate – may be a reflection of an inferiority complex on their part, refusing to identify themselves with typical black - "Negro" - Africa which is really where their ancestors came from, especially West Africa.

Not all all Rastafarians do that. There are many who identify themselves with people in countries such as Ghana and Nigeria as well as those in other black African countries.

But the tendency of some of them to identify with Ethiopia as their ancestral home – and their worship of Emperor Haile Selassie as God incarnate - is a delusion and distortion of history and reality. When he died in 1975, many Rastafarians did not believe the news about his death. They said it was a hoax.

Their glorification of Haile Selassie also has to do with the fact that he was the emperor of the only country in sub-Saharan Africa that was never colonized. Many Rastafarians also learn Amharic, a Semitic language which is also the official language of Ethiopia. The majority of Ethiopians themselves are Semitic.

Still, no slaves were taken from Ethiopia and shipped to the Americas. And the racial identity of the vast majority of

Ethiopians has nothing to do with the identity of Yorubas, Igbos, Ashantis, Ewes, the Ga, the Mandinka, the Wolof, the Mende, the Bakongo, the Ovimbundu and many other black African ethnic groups from which slaves were taken.

But that does not mean that Ethiopians are not Africans. They are Africans, although many of them may not want to identify with "Negro" Africans; a problem which has existed for quite some time and which even some people outside Africa have noticed.

They include African Americans, some of whom had a rude awakening when they identified with and supported Ethiopia when the country was invaded by Mussolini in October 1935 and occupied until the Italian invaders were driven out by the Allied forces in 1941. As Rupert Emerson and Martin Kilson, professors at Harvard University, stated in their essay "The American Dilemma in A Changing World: The Rise of Africa and The Negro American" in *The Negro American*:

> The Italian attack on Ethiopia in 1935, it has been said, had the effect of giving large numbers of Negroes a sense of involvement in world events for the first time, even though the Ethiopians were then by no means sure that they wanted to be counted among black Africans....(But) some Negroes no doubt still repudiate Africa. - (Rupert Emerson and Martin Kilson, *Negro American*, Beacon Press, 1967, p. 642).

And even though it is only a minority of Afro-Caribbeans who identify with Ethiopia as their homeland – in spite of all the evidence to the contrary including their "Negro" physical features you don't find among most Ethiopians – the mere fact that some of them do raises serious questions about the racial pride of some people of "Negro" origin.

It is a sentiment reminiscent of what the Black Muslims and their leaders including Elijah Muhammad himself "believed" in terms of their origin.

Elijah Muhammad said black people in the United States, not just the members of the Nation of Islam, were "Asiatics" and originally came from Morocco in North Africa. It was a deliberate attempt to disassociate and distance themselves from black Africa which is where they actually originated. They were ashamed of their roots deeply rooted in black Africa south of the Sahara, not in North Africa.

Not all of them shared this "belief." Malcolm X was one of them and was blunt about it especially after he left the Nation of Islam. As he said in one of his recorded speeches which was also published in *Malcolm X Speaks*:

> Having complete control over Africa, the colonial powers of Europe projected the image of Africa negatively. They always project Africa in a negative light: jungle. savages, cannibals, nothing civilized.
> Why then naturally it was so negative that it was negative to you and me, and you and I began to hate it. We didn't want anybody calling us Africans. In hating Africa and in hating the Africans we ended up hating ourselves, without even realizing it. Because you can't hate the roots of a tree and not hate the tree. You can't hate your origin and not end up hating yourself. You can't hate Africa and not hate yourself.
> You show me one of these people over here who has been thoroughly brainwashed and has a negative attitude toward Africa, and I'll show you one who has a negative attitude toward himself. You can't have a positive attitude toward yourself and a negative attitude toward Africa at the same time.
> To the same degree that your understanding of and attitude toward Africa become positive, you'll find that your understanding of and your attitude toward yourself will also become positive. And this is what the white man knows.
> So they very skillfully make you and me hate our African identity, our African characteristics.

Whether we like it or not, we have to admit and be brutally frank that there is a tendency among some blacks in the diaspora and even in Africa itself to admire certain features, what have been described as "fine" features of Caucasians and of people like Ethiopians, Somalis and Fulanis all of whom are also sometimes called "black Caucasians" – with aquiline noses, thin long faces, light complexion, long necks and "straight or wavy soft" hair - as opposed to typical "Negro" or "Negroid" features: thick lips, flat or "squashed" nose, wide face, dark complexion, short neck, and "kinky" hair.

There is even a saying in East Africa among some Kenyans that if you want a beautiful woman, go to Ethiopia; probably even Somalia although it is not common for Somali – and even Ethiopian - women to marry "Negroes."

And among the Hutu in Rwanda and Burundi, you hear some people saying successful Hutu men prefers to marry aTutsi women. The Tutsi themselves originally came from northeast Africa, possibly from Ethiopia, although there is a dispute over that.

So, some people of African descent in the diaspora who may feel that way and admire "non-Negro" Africans like Ethiopians and Somalis are not the only ones with that kind of attitude. There are continental Africans who feel the same way. And even if some of them may not care about having pointed noses, they like that straight or wavy hair, and light complexion, the very antithesis of typical "Negro" identity.

But they are not the majority in either case. A higher percentage of continental Africans don't feel that way; nor do those in the diaspora. Probably the majority who had such an inferiority complex because of their "ugly" black African features have overcome that.

However, it would be unrealistic to say or believe that only a small number of black West Indians or black Americans are ashamed of their African heritage. Many of them are, just as many of them are not. And tensions do exist between Afro-Caribbeans and Africans just as they exist between Africans and African Americans and between African Americans and Afro-Caribbeans although in varying degrees.

In a study conducted by John R. Logan and Glenn Deane at the Lewis Mumford Center for Comparative Urban and Regional Research, State University of New York-Albany, some factors were identified which may provide an explanation for some of the friction which exists between these groups in the United States. As they stated in their report on metropolitan racial and ethnic change entitled "Black Diversity in Metropolitan America" published on August 15, 2003:

> Early reports from Census 2000 about the growing diversity of the American population have emphasized the large increases in the Hispanic and Asian minorities in many regions of the country. There are also substantial differences within the black population that are worthy of attention.
> The number of black Americans with recent roots in sub-Saharan Africa nearly tripled during the 1990's.
> The number with origins in the Caribbean increased by over 60 percent. Census 2000 shows that Afro-Caribbeans in the United States number over 1.5 million, larger than some more visible national-origin groups such as Cubans and Koreans. Africans number over 600 thousand.

In some major metropolitan regions, these "new" black groups amount to 20% or more of the black population. And nationally nearly 25% of the growth of the black population between 1990 and 2000 was due to people from Africa and the Caribbean.

This report summarizes what is known about the social backgrounds and residential locations of non-Hispanic blacks in metropolitan America.

Among blacks, both the Afro-Caribbean population (people from such places as Jamaica and Haiti) and people with recent sub-Saharan African ancestry (from places like Nigeria and Ghana) are distinguished from the longer established African Americans.

Highlights

- Afro-Caribbeans are heavily concentrated on the East Coast. Six out of ten live in the New York, Miami, and Fort Lauderdale metropolitan regions. More than half are Haitian in Miami; Haitians are well represented but outnumbered by Jamaicans in New York and Fort Lauderdale.
- America's African population, on the other hand, is much more geographically dispersed. The largest numbers are in Washington and New York. In both places the majority are from West Africa, especially Ghana and Nigeria. East Africa, including Ethiopia and Somalia, is the other main origin.
- Like African Americans, Afro-Caribbeans and Africans are highly segregated from whites. But these black ethnic groups overlap only partly with one another in the neighborhoods where they live. Segregation among black ethnic groups reflects important social differences between them.
- In the metropolitan areas where they live in largest numbers, Africans tend to live in neighborhoods with higher median income and education level than African Americans and Afro-Caribbeans. In these metro areas Afro-Caribbeans tend to live in neighborhoods with a higher percent homeowners than either African Americans or Africans....

Jamaicans and Haitians are the two major sources of Afro-Caribbeans in all ten areas in the table. A majority in Miami (61%), West Palm Beach (62%), and Boston (57%), and a near majority in Newark (49.8%) are of Haitian ancestry. Jamaicans are the larger group in Fort Lauderdale (46%), New York (40%), Nassau-Suffolk (39%), Washington (49%), and Atlanta (53%).

Washington, D.C. and New York have the largest African-born populations (80,281 and 73,851, respectively). The 1990-2000 growth rates exceed 100 percent in all the top metro areas for this population, save Los Angeles-Long Beach (at 53.5 percent).

Minneapolis-St. Paul saw a 628.4 percent increase in its African population, largely due to refugees from East Africa. In Minneapolis-St. Paul, Africans contribute over 15 percent of the non-Hispanic black population; in Boston, Africans account for nearly 10 percent of non-Hispanic blacks.

In the ten metros in this table, most Africans were born in West Africa (mainly Nigeria and Ghana) or East Africa (Ethiopia or in the "other East Africa" category that includes Somalis). East Africans are the larger source in Minneapolis (61%), and they approximately equal West Africans in Los Angeles-Long Beach (37%) and Dallas (40%).

Elsewhere West Africans predominate: Washington (53%), New York (69%), Atlanta (48%), Boston (60%), Houston (61%), Chicago (58%), and Philadelphia (53%).

Social and Economic Characteristics of America's Black Populations

It is well known that the socioeconomic profile of non-Hispanic blacks is unfavorable compared to whites, Asians, and Hispanics. Table 4 offers a comparison based on the 1990 and 2000 PUMS.

Less recognized is the striking diversity within the black population. African Americans have lower educational attainment and median income, and higher unemployment and impoverishment than Afro-Caribbeans and Africans. Afro-Caribbeans and Africans generally compare favorably to America's Hispanic population, while African Americans fare worse:

- **Nativity** – Over two-thirds of the Afro-Caribbean and nearly 80 percent of the African population is foreign-born. The percent foreign-born of these groups is higher than that of Asians. Not surprisingly, the percent foreign-born among the group we define as African American is small.
- **Education** – Educational attainment of Africans (14.0 years) is higher than Afro-Caribbeans (12.6 years) or African Americans (12.4 years) – indeed, it is higher even than (that of) whites and Asians. This suggests that black Africans immigrate selectively to the U.S. based on their educational attainment or plans for higher education.
- **Income** – Median household income of African Americans is lower than any other group in the table, lower even than Hispanics. Africans and Afro-Caribbeans have much higher median incomes (about $43,000), though still well below whites and Asians.
- **Unemployment and poverty** – Africans and Afro-Caribbeans also have the lowest rates of unemployment and impoverishment among blacks, comparing favorably to Hispanics. Their position is substantially worse than that of Asians and whites, but Africans' unemployment is not far from that of these two groups.

Attempts to diffuse tensions between these groups of African people or peoples – Africans versus African Americans, Afro-Caribbeans versus African Americans, and Africans versus Afro-Caribbeans in the United States; and Africans versus Afro-Caribbeans in Britain   - have not always been successful.

But that is not much different from the tensions and hostilities which exist among different ethnic groups in Africa itself.

Probably one major difference is that many people may take it for granted that black people in predominantly white countries or anywhere else in the world where they are a minority get along well regardless of where they came from simply because they are black or because they are a minority. That is not always the case. In fact, even some Africans from the same country – but from different ethnic groups – have clashed sometimes in the United States or they simply don't get along well.

As far back as the sixties, differences among these groups of immigrants were identified by a number of scholars, including Daniel Patrick Moynihan and Nathan Glazer in their highly influential book *Beyond The Melting Pot: The Negroes, Puerto Ricans, Jews, Italians and Irish of New York City* first published in 1963. For example, in this study, immigrants from Barbados talked about their strong family ties and how they worked hard and saved money in order to get ahead in life.

The implication in what they – as well as others - said was that black Americans don't save and work as hard as many of these black immigrants from the Caribbean do. And it is a stereotype that persists unto this day among many of these immigrants – the Bajans (Barbadians) and others.

But in spite of all these differences between Africans, African Americans and Afro-Caribbeans, many of them do get along well; also many others don't, frankly speaking.

Yet on the positive side, there are a number of examples of cooperation between them. For example, on several college campuses in the United States, Canada and Britain, African and Afro-Caribbean students have formed organizations and belong to the same student unions as an expression of racial solidarity and in pursuit of common goals including forging and strengthening ties with their brethren, African American students, and others. There are also many other cases of cooperation between these groups.

Marriage among them has also made families out of strangers, and may be even out of enemies, sometimes. And since they are all an African people, calling such unions "intermarriage" seems to be inappropriate, although some – and may be most – sociologists may have a different interpretation of this sociological phenomenon and call it intermarriage since Africans,

African Americans and Afro-Caribbeans are identified and defined as distinct ethnic groups each with its own identity. Yet, the institution of marriage has blurred such distinctions in many cases.

Whatever the case, cooperation among them is cause for celebration even if it does not always lead to marriage, or "intermarriage," among them to start new families. But there is no doubt that the institution of marriage can play, and has in fact played and will continue to play, a critical role in establishing and strengthening ties between many members of these groups not only in the United States, Canada and Britain but in other countries as well including those in Africa and the island nations in the Caribbean.

One example of cooperation and harmonious relationships between Africans and the people of African descent in the diaspora is cited below. As Carla Thompson stated in her report, "The New African Americans: African and Caribbean Immigrants Are Changing Black Identity in the United States," in *Black Voices*, December 7, 2005:

> For almost their entire history in this country, black Americans have been debating the primacy of race as a building block for community and social relationships, often taking a cautionary approach about its importance: "Not everyone who is your color is your kind," they would warn their children, or repeating the popular Zora Neale Hurston maxim, "All of your skinfolk are not your kinfolk," they would remind themselves.
>
> The wave of Caribbean immigration early in the last century, established a set of tensions between West Indians and native born black that persist to this day. But whatever differences existed seemed relatively minor in the face of a common history of slavery, racial segregation, and economic struggle.
>
> Several Caribbean immigrants and Caribbean Americans -- Marcus Garvey, Claude McKay, Harry Belafonte, Sidney Portier, Paule Marshall, George Padmore, etc. -- rose to high profiles in black America and remain icons today. Being black was defined by not being white.
>
> But the question of what it meant to be black was always a complicated one, and the neither passage of time, the end of segregation, nor the emergence of a robust black American middle-class has done much to lessen the complexity.
>
> And now a new wave of immigration is deepening the complexity of the issues. There has been a 67 percent increase in the number of US residents, who identify themselves as Caribbean-born and a 167 percent increase in those who are "African-born," according to the most recent Census Bureau data. And despite the fact that foreign-born blacks remain a small segment of America's

overall black population -- two percent for Africans and four percent for those born in the Caribbean -- their pattern of concentration make for disproportionately large impacts in certain places. Increasingly, black people born in the US are forced to confront black cultures very different from their own.

Take Nigerian-born Lola Adigun, who lives in the Atlanta, regarded by many as the capital of black progress in the American South. Whatever else she is. Adigun does not define herself as an American. In her mind, an American is someone born and raised in the U.S., with parents who themselves were born and raised here; someone, she says, who "can't be deported."

But she also uses the term to differentiate herself culturally from native-born blacks: "We have holidays for the Yoruba God. We have naming ceremonies for children one week after they are born," says Adigun, a member of the Yoruba tribe and a 10-year Atlanta metro resident. "When people marry they have a 'bride prize,' like a dowry. We still celebrate these things in America."

Many of the new immigrants are settling in New York, Maryland and Florida but many are branching out to areas such as Minneapolis and Atlanta which, for example, has seen a 285 percent growth in its African-born population.

African and Caribbean communities living in America are more apt to use monikers to distinguish themselves from the larger black American community: One term in significant use by both groups is "American."

Adigun say she does her part to get the groups together by holding gatherings such as dinners, housewarming and game nights. She believes that as groups interact with one another they will begin to understand each other and have an appreciation for their diffcrences as well as their similarities. "I like to learn about other cultures," says Adigun.

Adigun and two of her fellow Atlantans -- one black American and one of Jamaican heritage -- talked to *Black Voices* about some of the spoken and unspoken issues that color the relationship among people of these different backgrounds.

I am What I Call Myself

Self-identification is important to blacks brought to the United States by slavery. As the socio-political landscape has changed, so have the monikers from Negro, Colored, Black to African-American.

"African American" is the dressed-up term for Black. I think it is a good attempt to attach our African heritage to our current state of living in America," says Odell Simmons, a 30-year-old black American artist. "But honestly, it does not mean that much to me. It is about the same term as black."

According to Michael Lloyd, 32, a mental health social worker, of Jamaican heritage "A lot of (Jamaicans) separate themselves from African-Americans when it is convenient, like when it comes to partying or socializing." Similarly, Simmons doesn't let cultural differences deter him from socializing with Caribbeans at events like parties and soccer games.

"I feel well-received at times. I think most of my friends assume that I am Caribbean because I hang out a lot with them," says Simmons. "I don't really have a Northern or Southern accent and I talk real fast at times. Not to mention that I stay up on current reggae music and trends, plus I don't fake a front. I tell them that I was a military brat born in Alaska and raised in Oklahoma and Alabama."

Simmons says that their celebrations aren't any different than those of Southern blacks. "Somebody's going to play the host. Someone is going to stay by the food. Somebody is going to drink up all the drinks. Just recently, I attended a house party with mostly West Indian people and they had a spades table set and I was on the domino table. Music was playing. It felt like I was at a house party in Montgomery."

Partying with other black ethnic groups may be acceptable on some level but many say marriage is another story entirely.

"Most parents don't want their child to marry Americans. So dating is very limited," says Adigun. "A lot of my peers only date Nigerians."

"When you settle down, you may want to have a Caribbean chick," says Lloyd. "When it comes down to the end, you don't want to settle down with a Yankee because too much teaching is involved. If you are Caribbean, you don't have to explain culture. (So) you can move beyond that part and deal with other real issues.

"I can remember growing up was that my mother telling my sister to never marry a Caribbean boy only because they were very passionate people, plus I think we had a cousin that married someone from the islands and they broke up. It wasn't pretty," Simmons remembers.

Yet numerous African Americans have married blacks from the Caribbean and Africa. And there are increasing numbers of black Americans of mixed parentage.

Philippe Wamba, a half-Congolese, half African-American writer who died in a car crash in Kenya in 2002, wrote extensively about his experiences as a bi-cultural African American in his memoir *Kinship*. And J. Lorand Matory, a black American Anthropologist at Harvard who is married to a Nigerian woman, studies the points of synergy and disconnect extensively in his research.

He says many times blacks from different backgrounds collaborate and identify with each other when it is advantageous to them, especially economically. But still, he argues, each group views the others with a fair amount of suspicion usually based on entrenched stereotypes and limited exposure. Immigrants, he says, depending on their outlook and experiences, chose to resist or embrace assimilation into the broader African-American category.

A subject rarely spoken about in mixed company is the stereotypes that each group holds of the other.

Says Simmons, for both groups, Caribbean and African, it is that "they work all of the time," a stereotype popularized in the popular 'In Living Color' comedy skit 'Hey Mon.'

"With Africans, a stereotype is that they are all about the money. They all deal with bootleg movies and music," says Simmons.

Then there are the persisting African-bad-hygiene stereotypes or African-American derisions for Africans like 'African booty scratcher' or 'Jungle Bunny' and 'Island Coconut Eater' for Caribbeans. The Yoruba 'Akata,' which loosely translates to 'cotton picker' (also brutal wild animal) is a common derogation some Africans in urban areas reserve for African Americans.

According to Adigun and Lloyd among both Caribbean immigrants and Africans, stereotypes of black Americans are the same: They are lazy, don't take advantage of opportunity, don't take care of family, don't complete their education and are untrustworthy.

Adigun says that these beliefs are especially prevalent among the older generation of Africans. "But these ideas are waning, but slowly because it is passed down from generation to generation," says Adigun. "I don't like generalizations. You can't lump all Nigerians or Americans together."

Lloyd agrees. "Right now, you have a lot of West Indians that fit that stereotype," says Lloyd.

"I think it's unfortunate that most Caribbeans and Africans have a view that is shaped by the negative images put forth by U.S. media," says Simmons. "I feel there is no balance they only show negative and the negative images they show travels worldwide. So people in St. Thomas and Nigeria think we all behave like what they see on Rap City and MTV." Similarly shows like 'Tarzan' and numerous others have shaped the image of primitive Africans in the American imagination.

For many like Simmons, the bottom line is that no matter how we may view ourselves -- with all of our ethnic and cultural nuances -- it is the larger American society that will have a major role in determining our identity and ultimately our destiny.

"I feel that when you walk into an establishment not owned by a West Indian or an African you are looked at as Black. The bank doesn't care that you are half-Indian and from Trinidad, you look black so you are black. Dark or light skin, full lips and hips and curly or wavy hair, you are looked at as black," says Simmons. "(We) are too concerned with distinctions -- Blacks have been like this for a while. We need to stop because there are so many other bigger issues that are facing us as black people."

Those distinctions and differences have always existed and will probably continue to exist between these groups. But many people in the same groups have also been able to forge alliances in pursuit of common goals.

The best example in recent times when they transcended those differences was during the campaign against apartheid, especially in the eighties when the campaign was most intense. Black people in the United States, Britain, Canada and the Caribbean worked together and with other progressive forces in their campaign against that diabolical institution.

And I use the term "progressive" deliberately to make one important distinction. Conservatives always associate the term with leftist causes. Yet the struggle against apartheid was not a leftist cause anymore than the struggle for racial equality in the United States was. White conservatives were some of the biggest opponents of both and the term "racial equality" is not in their lexicon.

Whatever the case, there is no question that the struggle for racial equality has been one of the most powerful binding forces that has enabled black people in Africa, in the United States, in the Caribbean, in Britain, in Canada and elsewhere to come together and realize that their destinies are inextricably linked as one people of the same African origin.

Although among the people of African descent in the diaspora it is African Americans who probably played the most prominent role in the struggle against apartheid spearheaded by Randall Robinson, head of TransAfrica in Washington, D.C., it is worth remembering that the people of African descent in the Caribbean have played an equally important role in the struggle for racial emancipation since slavery.

People from the Caribbean also played a critical role in advancing the cause of Pan-Africanism from the beginning. In fact, some of the most prominent leaders of the Pan-African movement came from the Caribbean. Some of them also went to live in Africa.

The most well-known in contemporary times were George Padmore, originally from Trinidad, and Dr. W.E.B. DuBois from the United States. Both went to live in Ghana. And both died as citizens of Ghana.

They worked closely with Kwame Nkrumah, Ghana's first president. Padmore was Nkrumah's adviser since the 1950s and went on to become head of the African Affairs Department under him. And as Padmore himself wrote about the origins of Pan-Africanism in his most well-known book, *Pan-Africanism or Communism?: The Coming Struggle for Africa*:

> Although Dr. DuBois was not the first Negro intellectual to have visions of a Pan-African movement, the credit must go to him for giving reality to the dream and conserving its ideals until such time as it found acceptance as the basic ideology of emergent African nationalism.

The idea of Pan-Africanism first arose as a manifestation of fraternal solidarity among Africans and people of African descent. It was originally conceived by a West Indian barrister, Mr. Henry Sylvester-Williams of Trinidad who practised at the English Bar at the end of the nineteenth century, and beginning of the present (20th).

It appears that during his undergraduate days and after, Mr. Sylvester-Williams established intimate relations with West Africans in Britain and later acted as legal adviser to several African chiefs and other native dignitaries who visited the United Kingdom on political missions to the Colonial Office.

Africa then, as now, was going through crises. The old Bantu nations in Southern Africa were faced with racial conflict. The ancestral lands of these Africans were being threatened by Boers and Britons. The South African Charter Company of Cecil Rhodes was extending its tentacles into Central Africa.

Even in West Africa, the Governor of the Gold Coast, Sir William Maxwell, was attempting to turn Fanti tribal lands into Crown property.

To combat the aggressive policies of British imperialists, Mr. Sylvester-Williams took the initiative in convening a Pan-African conference in London in 1900, as a forum of protest against the aggression of white colonizers and, at the same time, to make an appeal to the missionary and abolitionist traditions of the British people to protect the Africans from the depredations of the Empire builders.

'This meeting attracted attention, put the word "Pan-Africanism" in the dictionaries for the first time, and had some thirty delegates, mainly from England and the West Indies, with a few coloured North Americans. The conference was welcomed by the Lord Bishop of London and a promise was obtained from Queen Victoria, through Joseph Chamberlain, "not to overlook the interests and welfare of the native races."'[1]

Unfortunately Mr. Sylvester-Williams returned to the West Indies a few years later and died.

The Pan-African concept remained dormant until it was revived by Dr. DuBois after the First World War.

Thanks to his devotion and sacrifice, he gave body and soul to Sylvester-Williams's original idea of Pan-Africanism and broadened its perspective. - (George Padmore, *Pan-Africanism or Communism?: The Coming Struggle for Africa*, London, 1956, pp. 117 – 118; W.E.B. DuBois, *The World and Africa*, p. 7).

During the same period when Sylvester-Williams was actively engaged in pursuing Pan-African goals, another Afro-Caribbean intellectual, Dr. Edward Blyden, was playing a prominent role in the quest for racial justice on the African continent.

Blyden was of Ewe origin, an ethnic group native to Ghana and Togo, and was a great champion of African emancipation. Born on the West Indian island of St. Thomas in 1832, he went to Liberia - via New York - in January 1850 and settled there. He was only a teenager when he went to Liberia and was educated there and became one of the most prominent Afro-Caribbeans involved in the struggle for African liberation during those days.

An Afro-Caribbean who played the most prominent role in raising political awareness about Africa among the people of African descent in the diaspora was Marcus Garvey, a Jamaican, who was also known as Black Moses, especially in the 1920s when the "Back to Africa" movement he led was most active, mainly in the United States. His organization, the Universal Negro Improvement Association, mobilized hundreds of thousands of adherents in pursuit of his goals. Besides the members, there were millions of sympathizers. It was estimated that he had a total of 6 million supporters.

And he had the biggest influence on an African leader who became the most prominent spokesman and advocate of Pan-Africanism that transcended continental boundaries to embrace people of African descent in America and the Caribbean. The leader was Kwame Nkrumah. He said the book which had the biggest influence on him was *Marcus Garvey: Philosophy and Opinions*, as he stated in his autobiography, *Ghana: The Autobiography of Kwame Nkrumah*.

When he became president, he also paid tribute to Marcus Garvey as a source of inspiration for him in the struggle for African independence and redemption of the entire black race. As he stated at a state dinner on Ghana's independence day on 6 March 1957:

Here I wish I could quote Marcus Garvey. Once upon a time, he said, he looked through the whole world to see if he could find a government of a black people. He looked around, he did not find one, and he said he was going to create one.

Marcus Garvey did not succeed. But here today the work of Rousseau, the work of Marcus Garvey, the work of Aggrey, the work of Caseley Hayford, the work of these illustrious men who have gone before us, has come to reality at this present moment....

There exists a firm bond of sympathy between us and the Negro peoples of the Americas. The ancestors of so many of them come from this country. Even today in the West Indies, it is possible to hear words and phrases which come from various languages of the Gold Coast. - (Nkrumah, *I Speak of Freedom: A Statement of African Ideology*, New York, 1961, pp. 107, and 96; see also Nkrumah, *Autobiography*, p. 45).

Ties between Africa and the West Indies assumed another dimension when a significant number of Afro-Caribbeans migrated to West Africa and settled in Liberia and Sierra Leone through the years. Some also settled in Ghana and The Gambia; their settlement also facilitated by the fact that all these were English-speaking countries, and British colonies except Liberia which was founded by American abolitionists of the American Colonization Society.

And the Liberian governments, dominated by Americo-Liberians for 150 years since the founding of Liberia until 1980 when the last True Whig Party government was overthrown by soldiers who were members of the indigenous tribes, had a policy of encouraging Afro-Caribbeans to emigrate from the West Indies and settle in Liberia. It was vigorously pursued by President William Tubman in the 1950s.

Other people from the Caribbean have also established strong ties with Africa through the years. Some of them have also played a major role in the struggle for racial equality in the United States. They include Stokely Carmichael (Kwame Ture), originally from Trinidad, who first settled in the United States with his family and became a citizen. He later moved to Guinea where he lived for 30 years until his death in 1998.

Others include Louis Farrakhan, leader of the black Nation of Islam; Roy Innis who was director of Congress of Racial Equality (CORE) in the United States; Harry Belafonte, Sydney Poitier and many others.

Farrakhan was active in the Nation of Islam since the 1950s, while Belafonte and Poitier were actively involved in the civil rights movement with Dr. Martin Luther King.

Even Malcolm X had ties to the Caribbean. His mother came from Grenada. His father came from Georgia, a southern state in the United States, which was also the home state of Dr. Martin Luther King.

So, there is a history of involvement by many people from the Caribbean in the struggle for African redemption and in the quest for racial equality in the United States; an involvement that has helped to establish strong ties between Afro-Caribbeans, Africans and African Americans in pursuit of common causes and racial solidarity in a number of areas.

But much more needs to be done individually and collectively to overcome differences and stereotypes which impede progress towards unity.

Tensions which exist between many members of these groups, and lack of cooperation in a number of areas critical to our collective well-being, is more than enough evidence showing that we still have a long, long way to go in our quest for unity and racial solidarity.

Chapter Three:

Relations Between Africans and Afro-Caribbeans in Britain

RELATIONS between Africans and black people from the Caribbean living in Britain have through the years been characterised by contradictions: cooperation and conflict.

In recent years tensions between the two groups have assumed another dimension with the involvement of some leading figures from both communities addressing the subject and sometimes taking opposite sides instead of creating a united front to confront the problem.

In many cases, individual and even communal relations between the two are generally good. But that does not mean that serious problems don't exist in their relations. This was highlighted by a report on the BBC Caribbean News entitled "The African Caribbean Debate," 26 May 2006:

Abbott - Jamaican roots

Diane Abbott whose roots are Jamaican - she was born in London to Jamaican parents - has had to go to great lengths to defend and clarify the article (about Nigeria which she wrote and had it published in a Jamaican newspaper).

It has incensed some in Britain's African community who say black people from the Caribbean and Africa are different.

This issue has pitted Diane Abbott against Lola Ayorinde, a Nigerian-born British opposition Conservative party politician.

Mrs Ayorinde feels that for too long black people from the Caribbean have had the advantage over their African counterparts in the UK when it comes to access to social services, housing, and jobs.

"Anything that's supposed to go to us goes to the Caribbeans (sic). And the

Caribbeans seem to be in charge of any resource that are available" she said on BBC television.

Differences

She also highlights 'differences' between African and Caribbean peoples in Britain.

"We know by heritage they were once Africans. But those of us who came from Africa we clearly are different from them in terms of the languages we speak, we are different in terms of the priorities for our lives too."

Diane Abbott, who herself has been accused of stoking tensions between Britain's Caribbean and African communities, cautioned against divisiveness in the UK's black community.

Writing recently in a London newspaper she declared:

Abbott comments

"As a child growing up in the tight-knit Jamaican community, I was taught as an article of faith that people from Jamaica were better than any other country in the Caribbean (whom my parents referred to as "small islanders") and that Caribbean people were infinitely superior to Africans, who lived in mud huts and did not know how to comb their hair.

Meanwhile, on the other side of the world, African children were being taught how superior they were to Caribbean people, who had been stupid enough to get sold into slavery and were all thieves anyway."

"In recent years", she noted, "some of the silly myths and antagonism have resurfaced."

Such references have angered Lola Ayorinde.

Taken aback by fuss

Responding to the furore over her original article, Diane Abbott wrote that she was "...taken aback by the fuss here over a recent piece I wrote about Nigeria in a Jamaican newspaper.

Although I was anxious not to cause offence, I mentioned Nigeria's pervasive corruption and the tragedy of the Niger Delta, ravaged by pollution. The article enraged many Nigerians - partly because it touched on the raw nerve of African and Caribbean relations in this country."

Diane Abbott, the UK's first black woman member of parliament emphasises: "I think it's very important that everyone is proud of their cultural identity. But if we allow white politicians to play divide and rule, amongst the black community, nobody wins."

The Black African population in the UK is larger than the West Indian, and by 2010, it is expected that Africans will be the single largest ethnic group in the UK.

Although black Africans have made tremendous progress in

Britain in recent years, they are relatively new arrivals and were preceded by black West Indians who, because of that, may believe they are entitled to rights and privileges black African immigrants are not.

And that had generated tensions and even animosity between the two groups, compounded by stereotypes about each other as cited in the preceding article about the black British member of parliament (MP) Diane Abbott. As one Nigerian, Uche Nworah, stated in a post on a UK Nigerian discussion group Ijebuman's Diary in April 2006:

> Diane Abbot has now also shown Nigerians and by implication her many constituents her true face by her comments in a recent article she wrote for the *Jamaican Observer*....
>
> While Miss Abbott is entitled to her own opinion, it is important also for her to understand that decorum and public etiquette demands that she and her likes learn to make guarded statements, especially when commenting about other countries, especially when her comments (because of her political position) are bound to be either misinterpreted by others, and also if such comments are likely to ignite further the flames of inter-ethnic wrangling, in this case between Nigerians and Jamaicans in the UK who, if Miss Abbott had bothered to find out, do not necessarily enjoy a cordial relationship.

Tensions exist not only between Nigerians and Jamaicans in the UK but also between other Africans and West Indians as well; although the conflict between Nigerians and Jamaicans may be more pronounced than others.

Yet there are areas in which they cooperate, as Uche Nworah conceded in the same post as much as others have elsewhere. As Nworah stated:

> Diane Abbott...represents Hackney North and Stoke Newington constituency, one of the poorer districts in inner London.
>
> This daughter of immigrant Jamaican parents rode on the back of the 'black vote' to victory in 1987, by her own admission she owes much of her success to the support of Nigerians resident in her constituency.
>
> She was quoted to have remarked thus: "Nigeria has a very special place in my heart and I have so many friends there. My constituency in Hackney, East London, has the largest Nigerian population anywhere in the UK".
>
> These remarks from their Member of Parliament (MP) will surely gladden the hearts of Nigerians living in Miss Abbot's constituency, particularly Nigerians whose entrepreneurship drive the local Dalston market and contribute immensely to the local economy.

The emigration of black people from the Caribbean to the United Kingdom set a precedent in black migration to the British Isles. They were the pioneers of black migration to Britain, followed by black Africans.

West Indians were also among the first immigrants in the post-war era to achieve success in life in the UK. They started settling in Britain in large numbers from the late forties and through the fifties after the British government passed an immigration law in 1948 allowing people from British Commonwealth countries to be become British citizens and live in the UK.

Many West Indians continued to migrate to Britain after their island nations won independence in the sixties, although a restrictive immigration was passed in 1962 reducing the number of immigrants from British Commonwealth countries and others. And by 1972, only those who had work permits or family ties were allowed to settle in Britain.

The vast majority of the immigrants from the Caribbean or West Indies came from the island nations which were once British colonies.

And almost all the black immigrants from the Caribbean islands were anglicized in a way black African immigrants to Britain were not. After centuries of separation from Africa as a result of slavery, they lost their African identity in terms of culture and became "black Englishmen and women" even in their home countries in the Caribbean.

A new culture evolved in the Caribbean which became a hybrid of vestiges of African cultures and British culture, as well as infusions from other cultures including East Indian and even of those – the Carib – native to the region, further separating them from Africa.

In recent years, the separation has become even more pronounced as the two groups invoke stereotypes to describe each other in a way some of them did not in the past, as they compete for jobs and resources; and as they continue to defend their separate identities to justify their own prejudices and simply to make a point that "we are different peoples."

They are separated by more than culture, African versus West

Indian, and they are no more united by their skin colour or by their common identity as black people than they are by their common African heritage. All that means nothing to many of them on both sides.

Diane Abbott was accused of stoking tensions not only between Jamaicans and Africans in Britain but also between Africans and other black Caribbeans with her article, "Think Jamaica is Bad? Try Nigeria."

But she was not the only one. She articulated a collective sentiment shared by many other black West Indians who have a negative attitude towards Africa and African in general. She also inflamed passions among African immigrants in the United Kingdom, and not just among Nigerians, many of whom felt vindicated in their belief that West Indians think they are better than Africans.

And there were, of course, Africans who felt justified with their own prejudices against West Indians saying, after all, "they are not Africans; we have nothing to do with them just as they have nothing to do with us. Each to his own."

One Nigerian, Nnorom Azuonye on the BBC in November 2005, described the conflict between the two groups as "unnecessary, often nonsensical lingering intra-racial tensions between the Jamaican and West African peoples."

He wrote that in his review of a film, "Echoes of the Sierra Leonean War," which he also saw as a sub-textual examination of the tensions between West Indians and Africans in the UK.

The tensions may be unnecessary and nonsensical but they define and shape relations between Africans and black West Indians in a profound way and in such a manner that to many people on both sides, all talk of unity – not only between Africans and Afro-Caribbeans in Britain but also between Africans and people of African descent in general – is no more than empty rhetoric and sheer hypocrisy.

The tensions between the two groups were highlighted in another report in which Africans complained about mistreatment at the hands of West Indians in Britain. According to the report by Leo Benedictus, "From The Day We're Born Till The Day We Die, It's The Church: West Africans in Southwalk," published in *The Guardian*, London, 21 January 2005:

Posh Daddy is the manager of the Big Choice barbers on Peckham High Street, a mirrored box of rumbling dancehall and clipper-buzz. There's a Jamaican flag on the counter and plenty of booty on the wall: it's as Caribbean a setting as one might hope to find in London. Posh, however, is Nigerian.

Posh is easy to pick out from his colleagues; he has the word "PO$H" spelled out in silver and jewels on a medallion around his neck. His mother made it for him when he was 14, he says. It must have looked huge on him at the time. Wherever one finds machismo, it seems, a loving mother is never far away.

According to 2001 census figures, the number of black Africans in London (378,933) has now overtaken the number of black Caribbeans (343,567).

The two halves of the black community often live close together, sharing shops, schools and history, and yet they have acquired a reputation for not getting along - nowhere more famously than in Peckham, the most mythologised of London's inner cities, which was once home to another Nigerian, Oluwadamilola Taylor.

"When I first came to Peckham we just wanted to be accepted by the West Indian community," says Posh - an acronym constructed from Paul Olufunbi Shokoya (his name) and Harrison (his mother's). He is remembering 1988, when a young Nigerian student of child psychology came to London on holiday, got a girl pregnant, and decided to stay to look after her. "I used to have a lot of problems back then," he continues, leading the way down into the Big Choice basement.

What kind of problems? "Very violent problems. If you go into one of their pubs and you check one of their girls, you are in trouble if they know you are African. They'd go bumbaclot and all that." (Bumbaclot, the acme of Jamaican swearing, translates literally as "arsewipe". Its real meaning is more like a slow, surprised "motherfucker".)

In 16 years, Southwark, and particularly Peckham, has been transformed into London's west-African or "Nigerian" capital - the term is often wrongly applied to all west Africans. In fact, the patois that fills Rye Lane every Saturday afternoon is mostly Sierra Leonean, the language of a community that numbers 15,000 in Southwark alone.

But not everything has changed in that time, and tensions between the communities still exist. "It comes down to personality difference," says councillor Columba Blango, himself a Sierra Leonean and former mayor of Southwark. "Even though the west Africans and Jamaicans share things in common, where the difference comes is in their method and attitude. West Africans, we have a more subtle, and perhaps a more gliding approach to things."

Posh Daddy agrees, and offers a colourful example. "If a Jamaican man says to you, 'Go suck your mama', you would get angry. It got me angry for many years until about six months ago, because I don't like nobody cussing my mum. But it's like with the English guy who says 'piss off' - he doesn't really mean that. You just have to know the culture."

The Big Choice feels like a community centre. At a table nearby, one of

Posh's friends is teaching two small children to read. The front room was all men, mostly Jamaican; the back room, with its own front door, full of women; and the scattered toys around Posh's feet suggest that this is the kids' room. There must be almost 50 people in this small building, each taking time off from husbands and girlfriends, mothers and sons.

"It is getting better," Posh says, shooing away a pair of boisterous toddlers. "Now, most of my brothers up there in the barbers, they are all eating African food like me. We don't eat with a fork and a knife, we eat with our hand. Before, they said it was disgusting, but now they are doing the same thing like us."

West Africans have a reputation as keen churchgoers, too. Is this true? "From the day we're born till we die, it's the church," pronounces Posh with some majesty, "except for people like me who pull ourselves out of it." With that, he excuses himself and rejoins the Friday-night rush.

At 11am on Sunday, the South London Temple, based in what look like converted offices on Rye Lane, has nearly 300 people in it. Rarely among English churches, it filled up from the front rows backwards.

The congregation is about 80% West-African, by the estimate of Pastor John - mostly Ghanaian, it seems. Suits are popular, but there is also plenty of denim and African dress, as well as one mountain-chested woman's "Mind the Bump" T-shirt.

London, the cynical capital of the unbelieving English, must be one of the least religious places in the world. Of those who chose to answer the census question, 1,130,616 Londoners (15.8% of the total) said they had "no religion". Yet, as the city continues to be Africanised, so it is being evangelised. Charismatic and Pentecostal churches like this one do things differently, and they have flourished.

Everyone has been singing and dancing for an hour by the time the main attraction, Dr Shadrach Ofosuware, takes the stage, but he thinks we're still not warm enough.

"Give someone next to you a high five and say, 'liberty'," he cries. "Liberty!" "Now give them a higher five and say, 'Libertay!'" "LiberTAY!" Surfing the wave, Dr Ofosuware begins his sermon - 90 minutes of high-energy religious standup, complete with audience participation, sweat patches and jokes about Ghanaian fishermen (an old staple, no doubt).

Ofosuware weaves a theme of respect and moderation, meticulously referenced with quotes from the Bible, and his flock keeps track in their own study editions.

Finally, a large money basket is placed at the front of the hall, and collection envelopes are distributed. A man nearby discreetly folds in three tenners before joining the queue. His family has had value for money.

Religion is one of the most important things which binds Africans together and assumes even more significance when they are far away from home, and amidst tensions, but even in times of happiness. It is also invoked in their quest for better relations with other immigrant groups, especially Afro-Caribbeans with whom they live in the same communities.

But equally and probably even more important is their common identity as black Africans regardless of nationality. Many of them tend to stick together, and work together, as long as they are Africans, born in Africa, and brought up in Africa. Hostility or indifference towards them by other groups including West Indians also unites Africans against what may be perceived - rightly or wrongly - as a common threat or enemy.

Tensions between the two groups exist even in prisons in Britain. According to the London *Times* and other papers, there have been clashes in prisons between Africans and black West Indians through the years and the situation is not improving. One of the main reasons for the clashes is that they see themselves as different from each other in many fundamental respects.

And that is only the tip of the iceberg. Prison is just one arena of conflict. There are many others even if confrontations between the two groups are often more verbal than physical. And examples abound. As Charlotte Edwardes, a Trinidadian, stated in her article "Inter-racial Tension in Britain 'At Worst Level for 50 Years'", posted on the Internet on 8 August 2004:

> Racist tension between different ethnic groups in Britain is at its worst level for 50 years, according to a television documentary to be broadcast tomorrow.
>
> Darcus Howe, one of the country's most respected commentators on race issues, says in the Channel Four programme that violent confrontations between West Indians and Somalis in south London, and West Indians and Pakistanis in the West Midlands, are now endemic.
>
> Mr Howe, who was born in Trinidad but has lived in Britain since the 1960s, documents a huge increase in stabbings, beatings, attacks on private property and street fighting between the groups.
>
> The film paints a particularly bleak portrait of black-on-black violence between Somalis and West Indians living in the Woolwich and Plumstead areas of south London. Even while making the programme, entitled "Who You Callin' A Nigger?," Mr Howe's film crew were attacked by a Somali "community worker."
>
> Later, Jobie, a 16-year-old West Indian, recounts how he was set upon by a large group of Somalis he recognised from his area while he attended an anti-racism concert in Greenwich.
>
> The damage to his skull was so severe that it nearly killed him.
>
> Thousands of Somali asylum seekers, fleeing the civil war, settled in Woolwich in the early 1990s. Tensions between the arriving Somalis and more long-standing West Indian residents have now boiled over, the programme

suggests.

Jobie says: "When I talk about them it makes me want to be sick. I think they are vermin. They are not a civilised people. They are black but a different kind of black. To me they are like dirt. We have to clean up the dirt."

Jobie feels that his views are justified. "I can remember one punching me, I can remember a brick hitting my head. I could see blood but I didn't know where from. I felt my head. I went down, and I went unconscious. I ended up in an ambulance."

The film-makers also show how Hyacinth, who has lived in Woolwich for 21 years, has become a prisoner in her home. She relates how one August evening last year she was sitting alone in her flat when she was subjected to a terrifying siege for nine hours.

"I could hear bricks coming through my house breaking all the windows," she says. "We were so scared in here. [It went on] until quarter past five [in the morning]. Glass was flying everywhere - I was lying on the floor shaking."

The incident was reported by a group of white boys who told police that the attack was carried out by 25 Somalis. Since the incident, Hyacinth has invested £800 in her own CCTV surveillance to monitor what happens on her doorstep.

"I don't sleep until 2pm," she says. "I am so scared they might come back. I hate the Somalis - they should go back to their country. They are a warring people. They don't know about peace, they don't know about love. They have no heart. Truly they are animals."

Mr Howe says he is shocked by her language, describing it as similar to "a racist thug." But he is also sympathetic - his director was "slapped around" by a Somali community worker "because we did not ask his permission to film his subjects". He says: "Of everything I have seen I find the West Indian and Somali [violence] the hardest to stomach."

He discusses the issue with a group of young West Indians at the Charisma barber's shop in Woolwich. They, like Hyacinth, are vitriolic. One of his interviewees, wearing a baseball cap and a thick silver chain, says: "I had a Somali woman call me a nigger. You say to yourself, 'Well you are not white. You're black; you come from Africa.'"

"Their life over here is much better than it is over in Somalia. It's better than the lives of people that live and grow up in this country."

Yassin Ismail, a leader of the Somali community, criticised Mr Howe's film, saying that it was an inaccurate portrayal of Somalis.

"They didn't get the story from both sides - the documentary is absolutely biased," he said. "There has been a lot of violence against Somalis. We have had a number of incidents where Somalis were stabbed, beaten and even shot."

The Telegraph reported last December on Mr Howe's research into racial tension between Pakistani and Afro-Caribbean residents in Walsall. The film, which will be screened at 11pm on Channel Four tomorrow, shows Pakistani youths in the town threatening Mr Howe and talking about "bashing" and "mashing" blacks and Jews.

Even among Africans themselves in the UK and in the United States and Canada, there are differences in terms of perceptions of each other and how they see each other's identity or identities. For example, some Somalis in the UK say some Africans and black West Indians call them "Arabs" or "black Asians" because of their different physical features which show they belong to a different race. But it is also a fact, not a stereotype. They are not Arabs or black Asians but they are not "Negro" either, or "Bantu," like most black Africans are.

Also many of them think they are better than other Africans – so-called Negroes or Bantus, typical black Africans – as has been sadly demonstrated by the brutal treatment of the members of Bantu groups in Somalia who originally came from Tanzania and Mozambique and were forcibly taken to Somalia by the Arabs more than 300 years ago as slaves. And as one Somali woman in Britain, quoted by *The Washington Post*, who felt insulted when she was called an African, blurted out: "Do I look like a Nigerian?"

She is not alone.

And just as black skin does not unite black Africans and people of African descent in Britain, in just as many cases, it does not unite them in the United States, Canada and in many other countries, although it also does in many cases depending on the individuals involved. For example, one Nigerian in the United States said she was accepted by whites more than she was by black Americans; a fairly common remark or observation among a significant number of Africans in the United States; to which many American blacks respond - "You just want to be with whites," or something along those lines.

But there is no question that profound differences do exist even among Africans themselves. And many of them don't want to mingle or associate with black Americans or with West Indians and vice versa. As one Somali living in Britain stated in her post on "Somalis and West Indians Beefing in the UK":

The only time I have problem with other Africans is when they call North East Africans Arabs or Asians, just 'cause we look little bit different from them. Other than that East Africans have no problem with West Africans, Central Africans and Southern Africans.

Check what this disappointed Nigerian Sister had to say about African Americans and their attitude toward West Africans, or their ancestors:

"Growing up in Nigeria, Lillian Obiara and her peers idolized aspects of black America — the vibrant culture, the dynamic music, and the movie and sports personalities they saw on TV. Some of Obiara's girlfriends dreamed that one day they might marry an African American.

But when Obiara finally came to the United States less than two months ago to pursue a nursing degree, she was dismayed by the lack of knowledge about Africa, the insulting comments about the way Africans live, and the hostility she encountered from some black Americans.

'Before I came, I thought that since they are black-skinned like us, they would be more open,' said Obiara, 26, of Long Beach. 'The reality here is very different. The whites are more receptive than the blacks.'

Obiara's views are not uncommon among many of Southern California's 80,000-plus immigrants from sub-Saharan Africa — the majority from Ethiopia, Nigeria and Ghana.

Relations between African immigrants and African-Americans pose a paradox.

Many African-Americans feel an emotional and spiritual attachment to Africa. Some give their children African names — Kwame, Kofi, Hakeem — often employing elaborate African rituals. Weddings in which the bride and groom don ornate traditional attire, often a melange of costumes from across the continent, have grown in popularity."

Many African Americans are probably more interested in African culture than black West Indians are because they are a minority in a predominantly white racist society. They are powerless and don't have full control over their destiny.

By remarkable contrast, Afro-Caribbeans come from countries which are predominantly black and mostly ruled by blacks. In Britain this has a significant impact on how they see themselves and even on how they relate to or deal with other people, especially Africans. It exacerbates tensions and fuels rivalry between different groups.

The rivalry between West Indians and Africans in Britain – and elsewhere - assumes another dimension when both look at each other from this perspective: "I come from a black independent country." "So do I."

What is also sometimes overlooked is the fact that the complexities, rivalries and tensions, differences and similarities which characterize relations between Africans and West Indians are a universal phenomenon found in all societies and among people of all races.

Even people of ethnic groups which share cultural and linguistic ties, for example the Zulu and the Xhosa in South Africa, and the Akan in Ghana - which is a linguistic group including ethnic groups such as the Ashanti and the Fanti - do clash sometimes.

And many blacks are treated as outsiders even in Africa itself, by some people, if they go to places where they "don't belong." As Rommi Smith stated in her article, "My Africa," in which he also discussed tensions between Africans and Afro-Caribbeans, on BBC, 6 December 2005:

> I was inspired to write about the interview with Abena Assenso, a singer who I met some time ago when she sang backing vocals in my band here in Leeds. Abena (means as many people will know - a girl born on a Tuesday within Ghanaian culture). I know Abena as Maggie, but she adopted the name Abena when she married Chaka Assenso.
>
> When I hear people talk as if all Africans or Black people are the same, I want to tell them that there are as many differences between us as similarities - like any peoples. Chaka and Abena refer to their household as triple heritage: Caribbean, Ghanaian and English.
>
> Growing up in a Nigerian and English household I was acutely aware of the tensions between some African and some Caribbean people. This was best typified in Trix Worrell's show 'Desmonds'. Anyone remember that? The relationship between Pork pie and Matthew is what I remember.
>
> Anyway, I was talking about the relationship between Africa and the Caribbean with my friend Margaret and again with the photographer who was with us in the States documenting the Dancing the Guns to Silence Tour.
>
> We were discussing the tensions that sometimes exist between Africans and Caribbean people - the photographer, whose parents are from Jamaica said that his mother will not accept anyone who tells her she is African. Likewise, another friend mentioned that she felt that Africans looked down on her Caribbean roots, that she was seen as less African.
>
> I know that Abena felt deeply hurt when she went to Ghana and felt as though she was an outsider and was actually called white woman by strangers in the village. She said that she felt that she was made to feel an outsider here and made to feel an outsider there.
>
> So, I wanted to explore that sense of un-belonging, being made to feel an outsider, that sense of being removed and having to find your way back in.
>
> I think it's something that every second generation and even third generation of immigrant families has to face, the fact that you are defined by the place you're born. And in many ways you create your own unique, different sense of African-ness. And that's how culture shape-shifts and in essence for me, that's Diaspora.
>
> Many times I've been in a room and someone has mentioned that my father was Nigerian, or that I'm doing this residency and people will look at me as if to say - she's not really African. It's interesting and funny really that a continent so huge and with so many different facets and countries could possibly produce anyone who has a reductionist analysis of what constitutes African-ness - but there we go.

I asked Abena about what different cultural traditions they brought to their home and the raising of their children. Abena straight away said that she had celebrated Chaka's birthday (cakes, candles, balloons, the works) because culturally it wasn't something that he did, or was a big deal in Ghanaian culture.... I should mention that Chaka's father was one of Nkrumah's personal guardsman for many years.

Cultural differences are an integral part of the problem. But there are many other factors which collectively constitute the problem, including the legacy of slavery.

For those West Indians who acknowledge and embrace their African heritage without being ashamed of it or saying that they did not come from Africa, there are those who accuse Africans of selling them into slavery.

They even want them to apologize for that. As one West African living in the UK stated in her article, "Not My fault You're Black and British," 28 June 2006:

> When news broke that an Englishman had decided to go to African to apologise for his ancestor's involvement in slave trade, I waited with bated breath, scanning the MailMetro section for responses from members of the eminent British public. I knew what was coming next, and I was proved right.
>
> As expected, black British people responded with vehemence, saying that Mr Hawkins (the Englishman, duh) apologised to the wrong set of people. If at all an apology was in order, it should have been to them, the descendants of the slaves.
>
> And then they went on and said the thing that got me fuming - the shit many black British have so far got away with saying: that we West Africans descend from the people who sold their neighbours to the slavers. Now I'm tired of this.
>
> I ended a friendship with a Jamaican girl partly because she kept saying this, supposedly in jest.
>
> Yes, I'm African, West African at that. My forefathers didn't sell yours; I'm sure that had they been at the wrong place at the wrong time, we'd be the ones descended from slaves. No one should have had to be slaves, but we were.
>
> This Jamaican former friend of mine went as far as saying that the reason my family could afford to send me to university in England is because of the money my ancestors got from selling their fellow Nigerians.
>
> I find that unforgivable and unbelievably narrow-minded.
>
> The problems currently facing black British people surely cannot be attributed solely to the few Africans that sold their people.
>
> Yes, your forefathers should not have been sold or bought like commodities, but it's not fair to direct your anger at me - surely this is further splitting up the black community. I can't help where I come from (and the effects of that culture), just as you can't help yours.

Andrew Hawkins did what he thought was right. I can pick a million holes in his decision to apologise for the actions of his grandfather, but I'll just say that he did it in what he considered good faith.

But how feasible is it to expect him to trace the descendants of the Africans sold - remember that these 'slaves' were split up and shipped to different countries.

Now, I've noticed a restored hostility towards me by a lot of black British people (even those who I previously thought had understood the way things stood), and I've even got some smug white people telling me that it wasn't all them, and black people **did** sell their brothers and neighbours, etc. (presumably to alleviate their guilt about slavery? I don't know).

The anger and frustration of this Nigerian immigrant feels towards West Indians for what she considers to be unjust accusations of her ancestors' involvement in the slave trade are shared by many other Africans not only in the UK but in the United States, Canada and elsewhere. She went on to say:

I have a couple of things to say to that:

If the white people had not come to Africa and suggested the sale of people to the greedy leaders there, slavery would not have happened. Period.

They appealed to the greed of a few individuals, and I refuse to carry the stigma of being some kind of descendant of slave-sellers, on account of being an African. If there were no buyers, there would have been no sellers. From the history of Nigeria, this has proved to be true. White colonists gave power to the most corrupt and greedy, leaving a trail of slime and unhappiness wherever they were found

Hawkins' forefather and his white confederates had the guns, which technically means that they could have carted Africans off anytime. It was pure formality when they gave money, or cowrie shells, to the few leaders who sold their people.

I find that some of the black British people are simply scared. They want to sit down in their comfortable society, make vague references to a motherland they have no wish to get to know, while looking down on the very people from the 'motherland' - Africans - people like me.

If ever they visit any country within Africa (one of the 53 countries!), they expect to be welcomed with open arms, but that simply isn't the case. It's not their fault. They've got the losing end - they're part of a society that doesn't fully accept them, but they're also descended from a continent that doesn't recognise them either.

But I still don't think I (or any other black person) should bear the stigma of the extremely few people who weren't my ancestors (I'm sure - I've checked).

If blacks undergo racism from whites, should we also have to experience it from one another?!

> On the few occasions during which racist epithets have been hurled at me, the person perpetrating the act was black - usually of Carribean origin or black British (usually looking down on me as if I'm some sort of inferior species of black, and I was most incensed at that)
>
> So let's stop attacking one another. I've had to treat black British people with the same reserve that I treat white people, perhaps more, because of their open hostility towards me.
>
> In every job I've had, behind the bitchy white woman cutting my back to pieces was a black British woman egging her on, talking about the 'dirty Africans' coming to take over their country.
>
> It's not my fault. I find it most unfair when some black people 'rationalise' the actions of white people, while displaying open hostility to their fellow blacks.
>
> If we are ever to counter the various forms of racism that still exist in the world today, then I guess charity needs to start at home.

Quite a few people responded to that, some of them highly critical of her. They were mostly people of African descent in the diaspora who were stung or felt insulted by her remarks.

Some of the respondents were not harsh in their comments on what she wrote but were disturbed by the tensions which exist between these groups of Africans and people of African descent. As one Jamaican said in response to that: "I'm a Jamaican, but live in the States. What's odd to me is that here, I'm reading about all these tensions between Caribbean blacks and Africans (in the UK), but here, Caribbean blacks and Africans are more alike to each other than to African Americans. Black Americans tend to hate us all (we take all their jobs, lol!)."

The issue of slavery remains one of the most divisive in relations between continental Africans and people of African descent in the diaspora, be they in Britain, the United States, Canada, or the Caribbean or anywhere else. But equally divisive is the image of Africa.

The negative image and portrayal of Africa in the media and in history books for years has contributed to the propagation of stereotypes about the "Dark Continent" among many West Indians and other people, thus helping to create and fuel tensions between Africans and Afro-Caribbeans and in a society that has very little regard for black people in general; a point that was also underscored by one commentator in his post on Ligali Forum, a discussion group of Africans and people of African descent mostly in Britain, in which he had this to say:

> While Jamaicans are ethnically African, culturally there is a degree of tension between Jamaicans and Africans....
>
> Africans sometimes refer to Jamaicans as Jamos....In addition to this, there is evident conflict between Africans born in this country (UK) and the recent migration of Somalians to this country.

Yet, whatever tensions exist between Africans and black West Indians in the UK and in other countries such as the United States and Canada, which they do, there is no question that there are those who have been able to transcend differences which impede progress towards unity.

Cooperation in a number of areas and other achievements by both groups as a collective entity – with common goals and interests – in a predominantly white society have not been overshadowed by these tensions; although it must be conceded that they do pose a problem in relations between Africans and black West Indians.

And it is a problem that may even have ripple effect beyond the shores of the British Isles, as does indeed seems to be the case with the inflammatory remarks made by the black West Indian member of parliament, Diane Abbott, who represented a constituency which includes many African immigrants.

Still, there is no question that there has been cooperation between Africans and Afro-Caribbeans through the years not only in Britain but in other parts of the world as well, especially in the United States, in the Caribbean and in Africa itself.

And there is a long history of identification with Africa among many people from the Caribbean. The most prominent was, of course, Marcus Garvey, a Jamaican, who inspired and led the "Black to Africa" movement encompassing the United States and the Caribbean.

The "Back to Africa" movement was one of the most important political developments in the twentieth century in the African diaspora in the quest for black liberation and racial sovereignty on the African continent in spite of the fact that it did not succeed in achieving its political and economic goals.

It did not succeed in repatriating black people to Africa. It also did not succeed in achieving economic independence for black people in the diaspora or in establishing a black government. But it succeeded in instilling racial pride in many people of African descent in the United States and in the Caribbean.

It also succeeded in raising and increasing political awareness about Africa among many people of African descent in the diaspora. and had a lasting impact on the struggle for racial equality in the United States. It even inspired a number of political leaders in the Caribbean, and to a smaller extent in Africa as well especially in the case of Kwame Nkrumah, in their struggle for independence.

And there are still Garveyites today promoting and implementing the ideals of Marcus Garvey. One of the most visible organizations some of whose founding members were influenced by Marcus Garvey is the black Nation of Islam which still exists in the United States today.

In contemporary times, many people from the Caribbean supported the liberation struggle in Africa when a number of countries in southern Africa were still under white minority rule. They may not have played a major role the way African Americans did, but that can be attributed to lack of resources, not lack of commitment to the Pan-African cause.

It is worth remembering that all the countries in the West Indies with a majority of people who are of African descent are tiny countries, and with scant or very few resources. In fact, in terms of potential wealth, the island nations in the Caribbean are poorer than many – if not most - African countries which are endowed with an abundance of natural resources.

Even Jamaica, the biggest, has a population (2.7 million) smaller than the population of many African cities including Dar es Salaam, Tanzania, a city with more than 3 million people in a country of about 40 million.

And in recent times in Britain itself where tensions and rivalries exist between Africans and black West Indians, a number of prominent Afro-Caribbeans have shown great interest in Africa's well-being and demonstrated pride in their African heritage as have many ordinary Afro-Caribbeans in spite of the conflict which exists between them and many African immigrants in the UK.

One of them was Bernie Grant, originally from British Guiana now independent Guyana, who became a member of the British parliament.

He was proud of his African identity, and his African heritage, and was profiled on BBC as an "African Rebel" when he died in 2000 at the age of 56. According to the BBC UK politics report, "Bernie Grant – African Rebel," 31 May 2000:

> When Bernie Grant was asked shortly before he died how he would like to be remembered he said "as an African rebel".
>
> People were a touch bewildered. How could someone who hails from the former colony of British Guiana, who settled in Britain and became the first Afro-Caribbean MP call themselves an African?
>
> Bernie Grant was born in Georgetown, Guyana in 1944. The son of a headmaster, Eric Grant, and a schoolmistress (born Lily Blair), he was schooled in one of the colony's best schools, St Stanislaus College, run by Irish and English Jesuit priests.
>
> **Self respect**
>
> Grant was very conscious of his place in history, particularly as someone of African descent living in Britain.
>
> He wore traditional African dress at the opening of Parliament.
>
> He was making a simple point. Your ancestors (read privileged white members of the House) took my ancestors (read African slaves) to another part of the world, we were forced to lived by a different set of standards, but we haven't forgotten who we are. This is not about revenge, it is about self-respect.
>
> So where does this African thing come from?
>
> Wind the clock back a century and a half or so to 1833. The official end of slavery.
>
> The first black Grants and Blairs moved off a sugar plantation called Blairmont about sixty miles from the Guyanese capital Georgetown. The plantation is still there. The old planters' houses intact.
>
> The forebears of the freed slaves would have arrived in British Guiana between the mid-18th century and the turn of the 19th century.
>
> The French celebrate Bastille day every year. The Americans whoop it up for independence day. The British celebrate burning treacherous Catholics like Guido Fawkes.
>
> **Identity**
>
> All these celebrations and the linkages people derive from them are about identity and nationhood.
>
> In many parts of the Caribbean, emancipation day is now marked by annual celebrations, explicitly recognising an African heritage.
>
> When the British Parliament took the momentous step of outlawing slavery in all her Dominions in 1833, Members of Parliament voted a considerable amount of compensation for the dispossessed slave owners. In British Guiana it

ran to £4,297,117 10s 6d as compensation for the loss of 84,915 slaves. That is the equivalent of £260 million in today's money paid by the taxpayer.

Colonel James Blair would have received a handsome sum for his 1500-strong slave workforce at the Blairmont plantation.

The slaves received not a penny nor an apology. To be sure, at the time, freed slaves were probably grateful for their liberty and other small mercies.

Healing wounds

In Bernie Grant's last intervention in the House of Commons, on 11 November 1999, he sought an apology from the Prime Minister Tony Blair for the part the British state played in slavery.

He even pointed out how his own mother's maiden name was Blair. The plantation owners at the time of slavery were thought to be from the Scottish Clans of Blair and Grant.

Grant was simply pushing his creed that healing the wounds of the present, needs a recognition of the injustices of the past.

He wanted a permanent memorial in London to the 'unknown slave.' A symbolic gesture to those millions of slaves whose 'stolen' labour built up a sizeable portion of Britain's wealth.

It is time to give black, and white, Britons a new perspective on their common history. A 21st century diverse society could be all the better for it.

There are many black West Indians who don't identify with Africa – let alone call themselves African - the way Bernie Grant did and others do. Then there are those who simply say they are West Indians but still acknowledge their African heritage. There are also those who say they are no longer African because they have been separated from Africa for so long, And there are those who say they have nothing to do with Africa – and did not even come from there – although their ancestors came from Africa, captured and sold as slaves.

Then on the African side, you have those who identify with Afro-Caribbeans and those who don't. Some of those who don't identify with them say West Indians are arrogant, insult them, and make fun of them, saying they are primitive from a backward continent. And there are those who simply don't accept black West Indians as Africans. They see them as West Indians, not as Africans.

There are also those who have nothing but contempt for black West Indians. They see them as criminals, failures in school and in life in general; and coming from broken homes headed by single women who also have children out of wedlock.

The list goes on and on. And it comes from both sides.

So, tensions will continue to exist between Africans and West Indians. Also many of them from both groups will continue to work together and cooperate in a number of areas of mutual interest as they always have.

Rivalries will also continue even if in a constructive manner for one simple reason: Africans and Afro-Caribbeans have separate identities, and different cultures, shaped by different historical experiences in spite of the fact that they have a common African heritage.

They can emphasize similarities rather than differences for mutual progress and to live in harmony. But they cannot change or merge their identities to create a monolithic whole. It is neither wise nor practical.

Even Africans don't constitute a single ethnic group, although as immigrants in Britain and elsewhere they are seen and in many cases see and identify themselves as a collective entity. But they still celebrate their differences as well as their similarities in a true spirit of unity in diversity.

And that should be the case with West Indians and Africans as collective - yet separate - entities living harmoniously in a multicultural society like Britain.

Accept your differences. But don't hate each other. And emphasize what you have in common which is more than just skin colour in a world which couldn't care less if you wiped each other out.

Chapter Four:

Africans and Afro-Caribbeans in Britain: In Their Own Words

SOME call it separation of Africans in full acknowledgement of Afro-Caribbeans as Africans including those who simply want to call themselves West Indians.

Others call the tension between Africans and West Indians – or Afro-Caribbeans – as a reflection of fundamental differences between the two peoples because of their separate identities.

The tension is manifested in many ways ranging from indifference towards each other, name-calling, backing up stereotypes about each other with "empirical" evidence, to outright hostility which sometimes leads to violence.

Some Africans sometimes blame their plight on the privileged status of West Indians in British society. And some West Indians contend that they are entitled to more rights and privileges than Africans are because they were there first and are more British than Africans are.

Both accuse each other of arrogance. The list goes on and on.

Here is what some of them have to say. It is a sample representing different view points in the African and Afro-Caribbean communities but does not, in any way, claim to be representative of the entire spectrum of the views, ideologies and beliefs of the two communities.

It is, however, broad enough to reflect the perspectives of a large segment of the black community in Britain.

It is also intended to be an attempt to facilitate dialogue between Africans and Afro-Caribbeans – or black West Indians – which may help defuse tension between the two peoples.

The views come from a black discussion forum, Ligali Forum,

whose participants are mostly African and Afro-Caribbean:

Djehutis Wisdom, 21 May 2006:

"I was watching the politics show on BBC 1 today and they had some African brothers and sisters on there saying that they are treated unfairly compared to "those Caribbeans" in Britain.
All of their problems were blamed on "Those Caribbeans" and they made sure to point out their differences with "Those Caribbeans".
They were talking about how Africans have worse housing than "Caribbeans" (As if we aren't Africans) and seemed to believe that it was the fault of "Caribbeans" instead of the fault of this babylonian government.
One woman even said "if we want to get change, we are going to have to start with those Caribbeans".
I don't know about anyone else but the last time anyone referred to our people using the word "Those" before speaking about Africans they slipped the 'N' word in there somewhere.
I wonder, with African liberation day upcoming doesn't anyone wonder how we as African people are going to further our fight for freedom if silly governmental tactics, like making our own people speak about one another like Europeans do, are going to work so easily.
You can find video of the show here:
http://news.bbc.co.uk/1/hi/programmes/poli...ow/4988944.stm#

Voo, 21 May 2006:

"I just posted something on that 'woman' (Lola) Ayonrinde.
We've been on her case for a while now after she appeared on the BBC morning news a few years ago declaring that she wasn't interested in people like Malcolm X and Martin Luther King because they are not part of her African (read Nigerian) history."

Mogho Naaba, 21 May 2006:

""Not African anymore?" So when did we 'West Indians' stop being African?
Then she starts saying things like "you say we don't comb our

hair and live in mud huts"...damn I did I witness two African woman having a professional debate or a schoolyard quarrel?

This woman Lola...She really needs to remove the African garms from her body and wardrobe and simply cease to exist."

Zoraide, 29 May 2006:

"I hope nobody jumps on me for this.

Firstly I do not agree with what this Lola woman has said and never will. I do not know if this has been discussed before on this website I am new.

Maybe she has had some bitter experiences with Caribbean people in the past.

At the school I attended in south London 89% black, I saw people being bullied daily for being African.(people often forgot about me because apparently I don't look "african")

My best friend was told to go back to Africa by a Jamaican (she had been in the country under one year) girl wearing an Africa pendant.

My next door neighbour called my family refugees and that we should go back home. He also called my sister a "coolie bitch". (This man has been in the UK since 1964 - he is black Jamaican)

Throughout my life I have heard people say hurtful things about African people. African booboo, African this, African that, making fun of African foods, clothing speech. DAILY.

I have heard people deny slavery happened and that Caribbean people "evolved" from the island.

I have witnessed countless times as people screwed up their faces in disgust when you mistook them for being African. Surprised when somebody pretty was African because African people are "ugly". At my school a girl who arrived from Jamaica was very dark-skinned and people at my school were embarrassed that she was Caribbean.

This is just my experience, its not the experience of my siblings who went to different schools or my parents who came here in the sixties and seventies when i think there was more solidarity.

I bear absolutely no ill will towards African Caribbeans (I was engaged to a Jamaican) and some of my best friends lol! are

Caribbean.(I tend to get on more with people born in the Caribbean, rather than those born here - I don't know why, I was born here as well).

I am just saying what I experienced and I know I did not bear the brunt of it due to my physical appearance. I'm just giving another point of view. I am in no way trying to "stir" up trouble. But just explaining that some people have different experiences.

Oshun, 29 May 2006:

"I am of Caribbean heritage myself!...

I can't speak about the children at your school but the children at mine all came from second generation Caribbeans and so were told assimilate or die....

If your a child and all you are told of Afrika is that it is poor and destitute and full of starving people then you wont identify with that if your parents and your grandparents don't. And remember colonialism has ensured that any notion of where we originally came from and who we were has been erased....

We need more conscious Afrikan teachers in schools and after school clubs because our children are slipping through the cracks....

InCharge, 30 May 2006:

"There are some second generation Caribbean adults who say, well, my parents are Jamaican, but I class myself as Black British (whatever 'Black British' means).

There is not just a separation from the African Continent, but they also separate themselves from their Caribbean homelands as well, which is doubly sad.

Personally I think it is down to parenting. I mean there was this Jamaican girl in my class at uni who now claims that she is Scottish, because she has a Scottish grandfather (who most likely was a plantation owner on the Island and enslaved members of her family).

Her mother does not strike me as the type of person who is strong on identity.

As for the Continental African community, there is still some antagonism towards the African Caribbean community among the first generation (for some of the reasons Zoraide outlined).

This still occurs among the second generation (to a much lesser extent), whereas the third generation are more or less completely blind to the disputes of the first two generations. They mix so much more easily than in my time at school."

Sankofa, 30 May 2006:

"There are Africans from the continent who do the whole blighty (bloody?) thing...a la... EKOW ESHUN...many more..
There are complex issues, and they should be discussed."

InCharge, 30 May 2006:

"True. Its something that has come in with the second and third generation. You would never see such rubbish in the first generation.

However, although the first generation held on to their identity, I still believe they went wrong by not doing enough to pass it down.

Other ethnic minorities (non-African) in this country, despite some their negative points, don't seem compromise on this issue."

Conscious Sistah, 19 June 2006:

" I was so shocked at Lola (Ayorinde) as you can tell from my earlier post. She was so eager and passionate about establishing/creating this divide between the so called 'West Indians' (and continental Africans), to the point that she was acting like a hyperactive child having a seizure"....

Didn't you find it contradictory, when Geoff was saying that he couldn't pick up 50 young people in South London who knew what African Liberation Day was, but when AP phoned up saying that he is an AFRICAN, he immediately played devil's advocate, and said that he could be perceived as a mad person by some by saying I'm African?

I know that playing devil's advocate is something that Geoff does, in order to bring out both sides of an argument, but I thought he would have been pleased in a way, that here is a young brother that has a strong sense of self identity, unlike so many others.

DID you here the text that came in and said "I'm not African and I don't want to be"?

All I could do was laugh out of shock.

The other caller said that he tells his children that they are English because he wants to give them confidence."

Blackberry, 19 June 2006:

"I don't think Geoff contradicted himself. I think he was right when he said that he wouldn't have been able to find 50 young people in South London that knew what ALD (African Liberation Day) was, let alone attended.

African Phoenix's (AP's) call didn't really undermine that point. The sad fact is that AP is the exception rather than the rule, especially at his age.

At 25 yrs, I find it a rarity to find guys that will describe themselves as African, instead insisting on employing the euphemism of 'black', and this can be those who have left Africa but just a few years ago.

I think Geoff (Schumann) was putting AP's contribution in the context of the environment that we find ourselves in and are dealing with by reading out the text declaring 'I'm not an African', because like it or not, I believe that this typifies the attitude of our people, regardless of age.

This shame pervades rampantly among us. Even those who claim to be proud and exhibit consciousness, talk to them long enough and you'll identify a very real discomfort with defining themselves as African.

Jesus, the nonsense I've heard on 'community' radio stations where this has manifested itself all too clearly. This ranks from the appropriation of Asians as 'genuinely African', having 'come from Africans' (and their religion) because of the so-called 'untouchables' of India, to how Christianity and Islam are indigenous African religions that merely manifest themselves today in perverse forms.

I could go on and on, but that would just depress me!"

Vintage, 19 June 2006:

"Whether you're African or Caribbean, we are both seen as the scum of the earth according to the white British people....

By the way let me say that NEITHER the Caribbeans nor the Africans are getting a better deal. So for Lola (Ayorinde) and Diane (Abbott) to argue (on BBC) over biscuit crumbs is plain stupid..

To make the matter worse last Tuesday my brother told me to switch to powajam, and I did, and what I heard was Doctah X adding his own spin on the events. It was disgraceful, hearing the foul, degrading crap that was coming out of this guy's mouth about Nigerians."

Blackberry. 22 June 2006:

"*Embarrassment* encapsulates my feelings more than any other on this whole affair. Did anyone get a look of the New Nation's **'ABBOTT TRASHES NIGERIANS'** front page?, They out did themelves with their sensationalist nonsense that week, it was almost like they were proud! I didn't buy the paper let alone read the article and didn't watch the clip of The Politics show until weeks after it aired. As I expected, I found it nauseating.

I do believe that Ayorinde does have some genuinely interesting points to make, however, the pride she demonstrates in being a Tory, who had the privilege of being Mayor of Wandsworth, a "predominantly indigenous" borough, compromises everything else that she says in respect to continental Africans in this country. Her so-called concern comes across as nothing but a farce, and opportunity to exercise other agendas."

Twang, 23 June 2006:

"Just to sidetrack a little the lady that was in the studio called Ebony that was suppose to be reviewing the headlines along side Schumann when asked what do you class yourself as? She was quick to say English and that her parent's were West Indian.

I could hear a little smugness in her voice as if to say don't

even go there with this African foolishness but then I thought may be I'm being a little over critical until she started to talk about how excellent T&T played and how they were unlucky to loose but not one mention of how well Ghana played even though they had won and most Africans of all denomination's were pleased and caught up in the euphoria of a 'BLACK' team doing well.
This, to me, exposed her true underlying agenda."

Twang, on "What's to be Done About Diane Abbott?" concerning her offensive remarks about Nigeria, 22 May 2006:

"Sadly she represents a large majority (of West Indians or Afro-Caribbeans in their negative views and perception of Nigeria and Africa in general). Just check some of the key contributers to blacknet, moderators included."

Umoja, 30 December 2006:

"I'm new to this forum but have heard about tensions between continental Africans and Afro-Caribbeans, for example between Jamaicans and Nigerians.
What is the cause of those tensions or conflict?
Is it rivalry, competition for jobs, etc.? And does it have to with the fact that some or many Afro-Caribbeans don't want to identify themselves with continental Africans and are ashamed of their African heritage, also because some continental Africans don't accept them as fellow Africans?"

The Freelance Scientist, 30 December 2006:

"Welcome to the forum, Umoja! I look forward to learning from you.
In answer to your question, my humble opinion and experienced is that animosity between Africans in the Diaspora and in the West Indies exists amongst a sizable minority, and amongst a certain generation.
I haven't experienced any animosity from African Caribbeans anymore than what I've experienced from Mandinkas, my own tribe.

Rivalry and competition for jobs? Aren't all Africans, regardless of where their from, in the same boat?

Those that are ashamed of their African culture? There are one or two Africans brought up in Africa who've come here and are ashamed of their own culture.

There was some girl from my country who I met several weeks - I tried speaking to her in Mandinka. She insisted on speaking English.

She tries to talk like the Queen of England, but her accent drops pathetically in flight and returns to her African lilt so she's got to stop talking and try again. I say, people like that are all around!"

Djehutis Wisdom, 30 December 2006:

"Nope, it has nothing to do with jobs or rivalry.

The rivalry is as a result, only from what I have seen of course, of the older generations believing in the propaganda about each other.

Continental Africans have been told about the sexually driven, loud, violent etc, Caribbeans (especially Jamaicans). Caribbeans have been told that continental Africans are savage, unkempt, sick, AIDS ridden, tree-climbing beasts etc.

These are the propagandas from Caucasians that the elder generations believe. They insult each other for this very reason. This is why many (not all) continental Africans call Caribbeans "jamos" (despite the fact that we do not all come from Jamaica) and many (not all) Caribbeans call continental Africans "bush."

For the younger generation, these prejudices do not matter and are not seen until the teenage years. When they are exposed they create a conflict between the family and within the self.

I remember in college (And I was naive enough to participate) we would sit down and outright insult each others' cultures. The whole African (including Caribbean Africans) populace would gather to do so.

This is because many of the younger generation have listened to the prejudice of their parents.

Caribbean Africans have the internal fight of knowing they are Africans but being rejected by their brothers and sisters.

Continental Africans go through the internal strife of knowing that Caribbean Africans are Africans but their parents don't accept it. As well many continental Africans like a lot of things about Caribbean culture, however they are torn between the words of the older generation and their want to mix with their brothers and sisters.

Many try to ignore the prejudice but are ultimately still attached to it and at one time or another take pleasure in attacking their brothers and sisters.

Anyway, tangent over, most of it is nothing to do with identification or jobs, it is to do with prejudice in the elder generation and internal conflict.

The propaganda machine that has created this is often ignored and dismissed as fairytale but I assure you it exists, at least from what I have seen in my experience in life."

This is only a sample of the views and perceptions among a number of people who collectively constitute the black community in Britain. It does not present the entire picture but it shows how serious the problem is.

Although many people in the African and black West Indian – or Afro-Caribbean – communities get along just fine, there is a significant number of those who don't.

Therefore relations between the two communities can be described in more than one way. In many cases they good, and sometimes very good; and in many other cases they are bad. And sometimes they are very bad.

History also seems to have played some tricks on the minds of many people in both communities.

Separated from Africa for so long, stripped of their African identity in terms of culture during slavery, the descendants of African slaves in the Caribbean became "West Indians."

Those who lived in British colonies such as Jamaica, Barbados and most of the other island nations in the Caribbean which were also under British rule, became anglicized. And years later, many of them settled in Britain especially after the end of World War II.

Because they were anglicized, it was easier for them to be assimilated into British society than it was for African immigrants, a significant number of whom – especially from

Ghana and Nigeria – also started establishing communities in the UK in the late forties and early fifties.

Yet, although black West Indians – or Afro-Caribbeans – were assimilated into British society, they were not fully absorbed, let alone accepted, and remained on the periphery of the mainstream; a fate they shared with African immigrants because of racism. But many of them still saw themselves, and still see themselves, as being more British than African.

Coincidentally, it is a view shared by many continental Africans who don't accept them as an African people even if some of them don't believe that black West Indian immigrants in Britain are really British in terms of culture.

Thus, while a significant number of black West Indians don't want to identify with Africa or identify themselves as Africans, you have an equally large and may be an even larger number of continental Africans in Britain and elsewhere who don't accept not only black West Indians but also black Americans and others in the diaspora as Africans.

Many continental Africans contend that people of African descent lost their African identity centuries ago after being processed through slavery and therefore are not African anymore; although you probably won't find any who would say their ancestors were never African.

This reminds me of a conversation I had with a highly educated African in New York City in November 1972 when I first arrived in the United States. He had by then been in the United States for eight years and had during those years interacted with many African Americans who were in those days simply called black Americans or Afro-Americans and even sometimes "Negroes."

He conceded that racism in the United States was still a major problem although things were better than they were before. So I asked him, "What about those who want to go back to Africa? Is it many of them?" He shot right back: "When were they there?"

It was in pointed reference to the term "go back" I had used in my question which implied that American blacks who wanted to go and live in Africa would simply be "returning home," their motherland.

His response had profound implications. And there were many

other Africans who felt the way he did and still do: Black people in the United States, in the Caribbean and elsewhere in the diaspora are *not* African! Case closed.

So, history has played some tricks on many people on both sides. There are many blacks in the diaspora who don't want to have anything to do with Africa, and there are many Africans who don't want to have anything to do with them either!

One of the most divisive factors between the two is the condition of Africa as an underdeveloped or "primitive" continent.

Many blacks in the diaspora feel insulted when you call them "African." And quite often, many continental Africans are stung by insults hurled at them by a significant number of black West Indians – and others – who call them "savages," "backward," "disease-ridden," "mud-hut dwellers with poor hygiene" and other uncomplimentary names.

Yet even those who don't want to identify with Africa or with continental Africans, they cannot change their identity as an African people or people of African descent whose roots are deeply rooted in what they consider to be a "backward, primitive, dark continent."

There are also those who identify themselves with Africans yet are ashamed of their African roots. They don't say so in public or in front of Africans but express their reservations privately or among those who share their views.

Then there are Afro-Caribbeans who are not ashamed of their roots. They are proud of their African heritage and embrace continental Africans as their own people. Yet some Africans don't want to accept that.

But nobody, including continental Africans, can deny them their identity as an African people. Their identity as an African people is a natural right. They were born African, and they will die African, regardless of where they were born. And that includes those who deny their roots.

Those who deny their roots because Africa is a "primitive and backward" continent should also look at history and try to understand *why* Africa is underdeveloped, a subject that was addressed by Dr. Walter Rodney in his book *How Europe Underdeveloped Africa*. He wrote the book when he taught at the

University of Dar es Salaam in Tanzania.

He came from Guyana and also taught at the University of the West Indies in Jamaica and was proud of his African heritage and called himself what he was, an African, although he did not repudiate his background as someone who was born and brought up in British Guiana.

He was an Afro-Caribbean, yet fiercely proud of his African origin and heritage. And although his country, Guyana, is on the mainland of South America, it is considered to be an integral part of the Caribbean with cultural and historical links to the island nations of the West Indies which were also former British colonies.

But he *never* glorified his former colonial masters, the British, the way many Afro-Caribbeans do, proud of their British "heritage" because they have been anglicized. He saw colonialism exactly what it was: an evil system of oppression and exploitation and said the only good thing about colonialism was when it ended.

Those who glorify the British also glorify colonialism. For, it is colonialism which produced them and made them British or turned them into carbon copies of white men and white women, although poor carbon copies.

It is that kind of attitude which prompted Eldridge Cleaver, a leader of the Black Panther Party (he was information minister) and probably its most eloquent, to say "our conquerors became our heroes."

Yet even some of these "heroes" or conquerors who are so much glorified by some of their subjects have enough sense – far more than those who worship them have – to admit wrongdoing. They know how the imperial powers destroyed Africa and her institutions and stunted her economic growth.

There are many whites in Britain who are not proud of their history in this regard: what their country – and other European countries - did to Africa and to Africans during imperial rule and even before then during the slave trade. As Dr. Richard Drayton, a senior lecturer at Cambridge University (his book *The Caribbean and the Making of the Modern World* was published in 2006) stated in his article "The Wealth of the West was Built on Africa's Exploitation: Britain has Never Faced Up to the Dark Side of Its

Imperial History" published in *The Guardian*, London, 20 August 2005:

Britain was the principal slaving nation of the modern world. In "The Empire Pays Back," a documentary broadcast by Channel 4 on Monday, Robert Beckford called on the British to take stock of this past.

Why, he asked, had Britain made no apology for African slavery, as it had done for the Irish potato famine? Why was there no substantial public monument of national contrition equivalent to Berlin's Holocaust Museum? Why, most crucially, was there no recognition of how wealth extracted from Africa and Africans made possible the vigour and prosperity of modern Britain? Was there not a case for Britain to pay reparations to the descendants of African slaves?

These are timely questions in a summer in which Blair and Bush, their hands still wet with Iraqi blood, sought to rebrand themselves as the saviours of Africa.

The G8's debt-forgiveness initiative was spun successfully as an act of western altruism. The generous Massas never bothered to explain that, in order to benefit, governments must agree to "conditions", which included allowing profit-making companies to take over public services. This was no gift; it was what the merchant bankers would call a "debt-for-equity swap", the equity here being national sovereignty.

The sweetest bit of the deal was that the money owed, already more than repaid in interest, had mostly gone to buy industrial imports from the west and Japan, and oil from nations who bank their profits in London and New York. Only in a bookkeeping sense had it ever left the rich world. No one considered that Africa's debt was trivial compared to what the west really owes Africa.

Beckford's experts estimated Britain's debt to Africans in the continent and diaspora to be in the trillions of pounds. While this was a useful benchmark, its basis was mistaken. Not because it was excessive, but because the real debt is incalculable. For without Africa and its Caribbean plantation extensions, the modern world as we know it would not exist.

Profits from slave trading and from sugar, coffee, cotton and tobacco are only a small part of the story. What mattered was how the pull and push from these industries transformed western Europe's economies. English banking, insurance, shipbuilding, wool and cotton manufacture, copper and iron smelting, and the cities of Bristol, Liverpool and Glasgow, multiplied in response to the direct and indirect stimulus of the slave plantations.

Joseph Inikori's masterful book, *Africans and The Industrial Revolution in England*, shows how African consumers, free and enslaved, nurtured Britain's infant manufacturing industry. As Malachy Postlethwayt, the political economist, candidly put it in 1745: "British trade is a magnificent superstructure of American commerce and naval power on an African foundation."

In *The Great Divergence*, Kenneth Pomeranz asked why Europe, rather than China, made the breakthrough first into a modern industrial economy. To his two answers - abundant coal and New World colonies - he should have added access to west Africa.

For, the colonial Americas were more Africa's creation than Europe's: before 1800, far more Africans than Europeans crossed the Atlantic. New World slaves were vital too, strangely enough, for European trade in the east. For, merchants needed precious metals to buy Asian luxuries, returning home with profits in the form of textiles; only through exchanging these cloths in Africa for slaves to be sold in the New World could Europe obtain new gold and silver to keep the system moving.

East Indian companies led ultimately to Europe's domination of Asia and its 19th-century humiliation of China.

Africa not only underpinned Europe's earlier development. Its palm oil, petroleum, copper, chromium, platinum and in particular gold were and are crucial to the later world economy. Only South America, at the zenith of its silver mines, outranks Africa's contribution to the growth of the global bullion supply.

The guinea coin paid homage in its name to the west African origins of one flood of gold. By this standard, the British pound since 1880 should have been rechristened the rand, for, Britain's prosperity and its currency stability depended on South Africa's mines.

I would wager that a large share of that gold in the IMF's vaults which was supposed to pay for Africa's debt relief had originally been stolen from that continent.

There are many who like to blame Africa's weak governments and economies, famines and disease on its post-1960 leadership. But the fragility of contemporary Africa is a direct consequence of two centuries of slaving, followed by another of colonial despotism. Nor was "decolonisation" all it seemed: both Britain and France attempted to corrupt the whole project of political sovereignty.

It is remarkable that none of those in Britain who talk about African dictatorship and kleptocracy seem aware that Idi Amin came to power in Uganda through British covert action, and that Nigeria's generals were supported and manipulated from 1960 onwards in support of Britain's oil interests.

It is amusing, too, to find the *Telegraph* and the *Daily Mail* - which just a generation ago supported Ian Smith's Rhodesia and South African apartheid - now so concerned about human rights in Zimbabwe.

The tragedy of Mugabe and others is that they learned too well from the British how to govern without real popular consent, and how to make the law serve ruthless private interest.

The real appetite of the west for democracy in Africa is less than it seems. We talk about the Congo tragedy without mentioning that it was a British statesman, Alec Douglas-Home, who agreed with the US president in 1960 that Patrice Lumumba, its elected leader, needed to "fall into a river of crocodiles".

African slavery and colonialism are not ancient or foreign history; the world they made is around us in Britain. It is not merely in economic terms that Africa underpins a modern experience of (white) British privilege.

Had Africa's signature not been visible on the body of the Brazilian Jean

Charles de Menezes, would he have been gunned down on a tube at Stockwell? The slight kink of the hair, his pale beige skin, broadcast something misread by police as foreign danger. In that sense, his shooting was the twin of the axe murder of Anthony Walker in Liverpool, and of the more than 100 deaths of black people in mysterious circumstances while in police, prison or hospital custody since 1969.

This universe of risk, part of the black experience, is the afterlife of slavery. The reverse of the medal is what WEB DuBois called the "wage of whiteness", the world of safety, trustworthiness, welcome that those with pale skins take for granted. The psychology of racism operates even among those who believe in human equality, shaping unequal outcomes in education, employment, criminal justice. By its light, such all-white clubs as the G8 continue to meet in comfort.

Early this year, Gordon Brown told journalists in Mozambique that Britain should stop apologising for colonialism. The truth is, though, that Britain has never even faced up to the dark side of its imperial history, let alone begun to apologise.

That has been the fate of Africa. It is a continent that has been ravaged for centuries because of the greed of the imperial powers who, ironically, are glorified and even worshiped by some of their victims. They include a significant number of Afro-Caribbeans - continental Africans as well - who are ashamed of their heritage deeply rooted in Africa.

It is a continent that has suffered so much at the hands of foreigners who invaded our motherland as if it belonged to nobody.

There is no other continent where it has been so easy for foreigners to take what does not belong to them. And there is no other continent that has suffered so much.

It is a point underscored even by other victims of the imperial powers although they are not African. As Indian Prime Minister Jawaharlal Nehru, whose country was a victim of imperial conquest and greed, stated in his article "Portuguese Colonialism: An Anachronism" published in *African Quarterly*, October-December 1961 (p. 9):

Reading throughout history I think the agony of the African continent...has not been equaled anywhere.

The greed of the imperial powers knew no bounds. As Dr. W.E.B. DuBois put it poetically in a powerful statement on the victimization of non-white peoples to enrich the white races in his monumental study *Black Reconstruction in America 1860 – 1880*:

> Immediately in Africa a black back runs red with the blood of the lash; in India, a brown girl is raped; in China a coolie starves; in Alabama seven darkies are more than lynched; while in London the white limbs of a prostitute are hung with jewel and silk. - (W.E.B. DuBois, *Black Reconstruction*, p. 728).

One would think that such a long history of common oppression and suffering would be more than enough to enable even some of the most hardened souls among Africans and the people of African descent to look beyond whatever differences they have in order to establish and build strong ties to pursue and achieve common goals.

It should also be more than enough to enable critics of Africa, and those who make fun of Africa as a "backward" continent, to look at the continent from a balanced perspective and understand *why* it is so "backward."

This is a continent which lost millions of people during the slave trade. And it has never fully recovered from the devastation wrought during that period which spanned centuries. Then came colonialism which also devastated the continent in more than one way.

Dr. W.E.B. DuBois, again, put it in a proper historical context when he stated with magnificent eloquence in his searing indictment against Europe in his book *Dark Water:Voices from Within the Veil*:

> The indictment of Africa against Europe is grave. For four hundred years white Europe was the chief support of that trade in human beings which first and last robbed Africa of a hundred million human beings, transformed the face of her social life, overthrew organized government, distorted ancient history, and snuffed out the lights of cultural development.
>
> Today instead of removing laborers from Africa to distant slavery, industry built on a new slavery approaches Africa to deprive the natives of their land, to force them to toil, and to reap all the profit for the white world. - (W.E.B. DuBois, *Dark Water*, pp. 57 - 58).

It may take history to remind many Africans and the people of African descent of their common destiny in a world that is still dominated by their conquerors. Then may be they will understand the imperative need for unity and racial solidarity in a hostile world.

And may be even those who are ashamed of their African identity and origin will be able to appreciate their intrinsic worth as human beings inferior to nobody; instead of being ashamed of what they are simply because they were conquered and humiliated by the very same people some of them still glorify so much.

History will then have served its purpose as a redemptive force to free them from psychological bondage.

Appendix I:

Chilly Coexistence: Africans and African Americans in the Bronx

Oscar Johnson

IT IS easy for African immigrants who increasingly call the Bronx home to "just get along" with their American-born black neighbors. But it is a chilly coexistence - a fact both sides acknowledge from across a subtle yet vast cultural divide.

True, a certain kinship is noted. "We see them as the same," said the Rev. Michael Aggrey, 38, a visiting Catholic priest from Ghana who serves a growing congregation of Ghanaians in the West Bronx. "We used to have the same culture."

Indeed. The new immigrants and the descendents of those once imported by force share African origins. They both fit into America's "black" racial category, and often scrape by on low incomes.

But African immigrants differ from their black predecessors, not only culturally, but in experience and perspective. Those differences are rarely discussed but widely understood to be at the root of a great divide.

Like a dozen African immigrants and African Americans who in interviews were pressed about their lack of relationships, Aggrey evinced a diplomacy that eventually gave way to candor.

While some African Americans are "very nice," he said, "the difference is the way we have been raised. The few African Americans I have interacted with are embittered with the past."

Aggrey's candor soon revealed bewilderment. "Why are the African Americans so into sports?" he asked. "We can go higher.

We can make education our priority. But if we are into basketball they (whites) can still be in control."

G. Ofori Anor, 50, a Ghanaian immigrant who moved to the Bronx 14 years ago, echoes Aggrey. Sober in spirit and conservatively casual in dress, he is the editor of Asante, a monthly newspaper. He said he renounced his first, or "Christian" name, but keeps the initial "G" in honor of his father who named him.

According to Anor, some aspects of African culture "embarrass" American blacks because the practices appear primitive to those used to more European standards.

He said this embarrassment causes some black Americans to distance themselves from anything - or anyone - who is explicitly African.

"On our side," Anor said, "we don't understand the way it appears that African Americans treat one another: Black on black crime - especially the youth killing themselves.

Recalling a visit to a largely African-American housing project, he lamented "the propensity for African Americans to run down their own neighborhood in protest." Someone had urinated in the building elevator, he said. "If you are really mad at the white man why don't you pee in his elevator? He doesn't ride in this one - you do."

For those more aligned with the African-American experience, such as Jalani Ja Lion, a walnut-hued Rastafarian who claims Cherokee and West Indian lineage, there is another perception.

"Africans come here and they are under a lot of misconceptions that African Americans are losers" and don't take advantage of opportunities, said Ja Lion, who sells incense, scented oils and other sundries from a folding table near Jerome Avenue. "But not everything here is a bed of roses. As long as there's a cultural barrier it's going to breed ignorance."

In the last decade there has been ample opportunity for cultural barriers to arise among black people in the Bronx. More than 1,600 Ghanaians now immigrate annually to the city - a 380 percent increase since the early 1990s - according to the city Department of City Planning report released last year.

Immigration and Naturalization Service data shows that in 1996, about two-thirds of those Ghanaians visiting the United

States (6,269), and nearly three-quarters of those naturalized (3,084), arrived in the city. Many have clustered in communities in Morris Heights, Highbridge and Tremont, making Ghana the No. 3 place of origin for immigrants to the Bronx, according to the report.

Meanwhile, city and community district data for the new millennium show that the borough's native-born black population - largely consisting of those traditionally called "black" and "African American"- is leaving the South Bronx.

In the last decade, many have migrated north to Coop City. Some have left the Bronx altogether. Now, a full two thirds of the borough's "black" population is foreign-born.

Neither the immigrants nor the native-born seem to harbor any intentional ill will towards one another. But both speak of distinctions, assumptions and de facto segregation.

"I wouldn't say the relation is cold but I wouldn't say it's warm either," said Randolph Hinds, 38, president of the African American Association in Coop City, and adjunct professor of sociology at New Rochelle College. He said one reason relations are tepid is because many African Americans feel the immigrants "are so clannish that they're not going to let you in...It's almost like an arrogance and a put down."

But African Americans have their own misconceptions about Africans. Hinds said some Africans are seen as "stupid" because of their accents and Third World origins, or deemed "annoying" because African women in Harlem often solicit would-be customers to get their hair braided.

Hinds said he once tried to get the association, which formed in 1978 to meet the cultural, educational and social needs of Coop City's black population, to change its name to one that would be more inclusive of immigrants and native-born blacks alike.

Hinds, the youngest member of the group's board of directors, said the idea was voted down overwhelmingly by the older majority. "I'm one vote on a board," he said. The others simply "are not as progressive."

On another occasion, he said he attended a meeting for a Harlem-based rites-of-passage organization for black youths. When it was proposed that the program include a trip to an African country to mark the youths' transition to adulthood, the idea met with opposition. "Some said 'We're not welcomed over there,'" recalled Hinds. "' They treat us badly.'"

Negative images and impressions both of African Americans and developing African countries in mainstream media helps perpetuate the rift, according to Philippe Wamba, editor-in-chief of Africana.com, an online publication that covers a variety African and African-American topics.

Wamba's father is from the Democratic Republic of Congo and his mother is from Michigan. He spent much of his youth growing up in the native countries of both parents.

"The main thing is ignorance on both sides," said Wamba, who has also written a book and several articles on the relationship between Africans and African Americans. "If the people know anything at all (about each other) it is very little, and it is very skewed."

Newspaper editor Anor, who acknowledges that one reason so many Ghanaians come to the Bronx is because of the borough's black population, has similar thoughts.

"I think there is a flood of information from our experience of colonialism and that still keeps us from understanding," he said. "It still dogs our relationship."

Ghanaian immigrant Georgina Tackie, 38, who manages the African American Restaurant, which serves Ghanaian and American soul food, has been in the United States for 15 years. The fathers of the single mother's four children are African American.

Like other African immigrants, she notes the differences between the two groups but has stumbled across at least one trait from the other side of the divide she admires.

"Ghanaians like to work, pay your rent and stay out of trouble," Tackie said, echoing almost verbatim how nearly a half-dozen other Ghanaians distinguished themselves from African Americans. "We are not outspoken. That's one good thing about us. Where you have Ghanaians living you never have trouble."

Then, after a pause, she added: "The only thing that bothers me is this guy Amadou Diallo. It's the African Americans that have stood up but it should be us - he is one of ours. I felt so sad that we were not particularly involved."

Tackie's afterthought is a common one among African

immigrants who have lived in the states for a while, according to Wamba. He said incidents such as the fatal police shooting of Diallo, an unarmed West African immigrant, cause many African newcomers to "consider going beyond our insular immigrant community."

According to Wamba: "It's an awakening to many Africans that, to many white people, they are indistinguishable from African Americans."

Similar histories of colonialism and slavery, or current experiences of discrimination in the United States and abroad can often serve as a bridge between the two groups' because racial inequality "seems to be a problem that all black people face," he said.

Hinds, the African American Association president, also finds something to learn from across the divide.

"It would be good to improve our relations between Africans and people here in America," he said. "We need to develop more of a world view, to not see ourselves so much as a minority.

"Because we have a breakdown in our history, I think it would help with our schizophrenic world view," Hinds said about the view of some black Americans that they are neither fully American nor African. "It could help with our social agony."

But Hinds said that only about 1 percent of his personal friends are African immigrants, despite the fact that he works with many of them. After some reflection, he adds: "My circle of friends could enlarge. It should.

"When I say it's only 1 percent, then I say: 'Maybe there's still a bit of work for me to do.'"

Source, Oscar Johnson, "Chilly Coexistence: Africans and African Americans in the Bronx" at:
www.columbia.edu/itc/journalism/gissler/anthology/Chill-Johnson.html

Appendix II:

Contemporary African Immigrants to The United States

Joseph Takougang

THE SEVERE economic difficulties, increased poverty and the political instability that have plagued many African countries in the last two decades have resulted in the large scale migration of Africans to Europe and the United States.

Unlike their counterparts in the 1960s and 70s who were anxious to return home after acquiring an American education in order to contribute in the task of nation building, an overwhelming majority of recent immigrants are more interested in establishing permanent residency in the United States. Although these immigrants continue to be attracted to major cities like New York, Atlanta, Chicago and Los Angeles, they can also be found in increasing numbers in small and mid-sized cities in Ohio, Nebraska, Iowa and Maine.

To experience the sights, sound and flavors of Africa without leaving Minnesota, just step into a Somali mini-mall in Minneapolis or an African shopping center in St. Paul. There are the sweet, pungent smells of Somali dishes, the vivid colors of African clothing, and the rapid-fire, foreign language conversations of Somalis, Ethiopians, and Liberians who moved to the states at a record pace during the past decade. - (Lourdes Medrano Leslie, *Minnesota Star Tribune*, June 4, 2002).

Africans permeate all aspects of Colorado life. They are doctors, lawyers, professors, engineers, students, cab drivers, clerks, security guards and chefs. They reflect some basic American passions: politics, the Broncos, day trading, eating burgers, even skiing. - (Sam Omatseye, *Rocky Mountain News*, March 19, 2000).

The influx of African immigrants to the United States in the last two decades has been phenomenal. According to figures from the Immigration and Naturalization Services (INS), the number of African immigrants to the United States more than quadrupled in the last two decades; from 109,733 between 1961 and 1980 to 531,832 between 1981 and 2000.

These new immigrants can be found in major metropolitan areas in states like New York, Texas, Georgia, Illinois, Maryland and California, to small towns in Idaho, Iowa and Maine. Even states like North and South Dakota that were only distant memories in the minds of many African immigrants to the United States in the 1960s and 70s have become homes to many Africans. For instance, South Dakota experienced an increase in the number of African immigrants from 210 in the 1990s to 1,560 in 2000. [1]

Similarly, Tacoma, Washington saw an increase of more than 800 percent in the number immigrants from sub-Saharan Africa- from 202 in the 1990s to 1,802 in 2002 [2].

Unlike their counterparts in the 1960s and 70s whose aspirations was to return to their respective countries with an American education and the skills necessary for the task of nation-building, many of the immigrants in the last two decades are more interested in settling in United States and building a comfortable life for themselves and their families.

This essay examines why an increasing number of African immigrants decide to become permanent residents or citizens of the United States instead of returning to their home countries. It also considers the various measures that these immigrants have taken to become integrated into their new environment.

Motivations for African Migration to the United States: The Hopes and Disappointments of Independence

At independence, Africans were filled with tremendous hope and optimism. For many Africans, independence was seen as more than just a period of self-rule and freedom. In their campaign speeches and rhetoric, they were led by many of the nationalist leaders to believe that independence would also lead to a significant improvement in their social and economic life, including improvements in education and health care, and greater employment opportunities.

Indeed, the institution of single-party rule shortly after independence in many African states was rationalized on the basis that it was the next logical political step to a more stable political environment and ultimately to impressive socio-economic development. Unfortunately, more than four decades after independence, the economy of most African states is characterized by grinding poverty, endemic corruption and high rates of unemployment.

This sad state of affairs is reflected in the salary scales of University professors in many African universities. With the exception of South Africa and Zimbabwe where the starting annual salary scale for a university lecturer in 1997 was over $10,000, the salary in other countries was below $4,000. [3]

Part of the reason for the declining fortunes of a continent so rich in natural resources is the authoritarian structure of the post-colonial state that continues to hinder the kind of open discussion and constructive criticism that might have fostered healthy and sustained economic development.

Instead of leading to a more stable society, the one-party state fostered endemic corruption by political leaders, nepotism, and the establishment of highly repressive and dictatorial regimes that suffocated free speech and had little regard for the human rights of their citizens across the continent.

The institution of such regimes allowed politicians and other important public officials to arrogantly drain the state treasury for their personal benefit.

Most of the money procured in this manner is either invested in real estate or other business ventures overseas or stashed in foreign banks in Europe, North America and the Caribbean. According to Whiteman, the Bank of France in 1988 alone bought back about 450 billion CFA francs (1.8 billion dollars) in bank notes that had been fraudulently transferred in full suitcases and diplomatic bags. [4]

The net result of such uninhibited corruption and capital flight is the fact that resources that could be invested in the various African countries to generate economic growth and create employment opportunities are lost to the Western Industrialized nations that do not need African capital.

Although mismanagement and corruption among African leaders have undoubtedly contributed to the continent's severe economic problems, a fundamental reason for the corruption can also be attributed to the lack of democratic governance and political transparency in most African states.

In fact, despite attempts since the early 1990s to institute democratic governance, political repression, human rights abuses and civil wars are still prevalent across the continent - Côte d'Ivoire, Sierra Leone, and The Democratic Republic of Congo are just a few examples.

In these and other African countries, the fear and intimidation that make citizens less likely to criticize the political process has encouraged such severe economic problems.

Apraku draws a correlation between an open political system and economic development when he argues that "without political pluralism, economic pluralism becomes very difficult to achieve, and without economic pluralism, private sector development becomes a very difficult and unrealistic proposition in Africa." [5]

Nigeria's current president, Olusegun Obasanjo articulated the same point when he argued that the continent's economic failures so far have been only symptoms of a more fundamental political failure. [6]

The situation has also been exacerbated by Africa's over-dependence on foreign markets for its raw materials and the continent's over-reliance on international financial institutions. Because Africa is unable to control the prices it receives for its primary products, it is forced, in most cases to accept prices that it is offered for those products by European and American buyers. Consequently, the prices it has received for those products have declined sharply in the last few decades.

The fall in prices have had direct bearings on how much money is available to most of these countries to carry out development projects or meet the salary demands of their citizens. For example, the per capita gross GNP for Zambia is reported to have fallen by about 27 percent in the ten-year period between 1974 and 1984, mostly because of a 60 percent decline in the price of copper, the country's major export during this period. [7] Meanwhile, Nigeria, which in the 1970s enjoyed a healthy economy and the status of a middle income country because of the high price it received for its oil, had by 1993, fallen to the ranks of one of the poorest nations in the world primarily because of a decline in the price of its oil. [8]

The net result of such economic paralysis and political suffocation is that, many Africans, particularly highly skilled professionals, have been forced to seek their economic fortunes elsewhere, including the United States. [9] In fact, a 1991 report estimated that one out of every four African in the United States was believed to be a Nigerian. [10]

And according to the United Nation's Human Development Report, in 1993, at a time when Nigeria's healthcare system was severely deficient there were more than 21,000 practicing Nigerian physicians in the United States. [11]

Recently the situation has become so severe that many of the highly skilled and trained professionals who had been educated in the United States and Europe and had returned home in the 1970s and early 80s have been forced to return to the West in search of better opportunities. [12]

Even some of the most patriotic African students who were still thinking of returning home after completing their course of study in the United States have become so disillusioned that many of them have given up the idea. [13]

This brain drain has resulted in the loss of one-third of the continent's skilled professionals in recent decades. While these highly skilled professionals are a tremendous asset to the further development of the United States and other developed nations of the world, the $4 billion that it cost to fill up the capacity gap created by their departure from their countries of origin continues to be a drain on the meager resources of African nations. [14]

This can only lead to further economic stagnation for the continent and its people. Commenting on the impact that the departure of these highly trained professionals is having on Africa, Dei and Asgharzadah note that:

The immediate effect of such an exodus on institutions of higher learning, research, and scientific work will surely be felt in that the brain drain deprives the African institutions of cutting-edge technological and scientific research that employs highly talented scientists and researchers.

The exodus of highly talented from Africa also means the transfer of considerable amount of money, assets, and funds. Every African who takes money from Africa and spends it abroad fails to help Africa financially, economically, and commercially. Likewise, every African who makes money abroad fails to help Africa's commercial or economic development. [15]

Although Africa's rather desperate economic and political future have been important factors for recent large-scale migration to the United States, it could be argued that the apparent relaxation of the United States' immigration policy has also been very helpful. [16]

Two policies in particular are worth mentioning: the 1986 Immigration Reform and Control Act and the Diversity Visa Program that was introduced as part of the 1990 Immigration Act. While the 1986 Act made it easier for undocumented immigrants, including those from Africa then living in the United States to become permanent residents, the Diversity Visa Program, which was aimed at promoting immigration from hitherto underrepresented countries and regions of the world allowed up to 50,000 "qualified" Africans annually to migrate to the United States through a lottery process.

At the same time that new opportunities for immigration to the United States were occurring, the slumping European economy, especially since the 1990s, and tighter immigration by many European countries, including Great Britain and France that had been the traditional areas of immigrants from Africa, have made the United States even more attractive to African immigrants. [17]

These changes have resulted in a significant increase in the number of African immigrants to the United States. For instance, the number of African immigrants to the United States in 1996 was 52, 889. That number was almost double the 26,716 that had entered the country in 1994. [18]

In fact, the "new" African immigrants to the United States no longer come only from former English-speaking colonies-as had been the case for decades since those from none English-speaking often found it difficult to learn a new language- but include immigrants from former Portuguese, Spanish and French colonies. According to the New York Department of City Planning, there were about 2,000 immigrants from Senegal - a former French colony in 2002. [19]

These men and women, some with very little education are willing to do anything to achieve the American dream. Unlike their counterparts in the 1960s and 70s, who always had the vision of returning home after completing their course of study and were therefore reluctant to become United States citizens, the new immigrants are quick to apply for citizenship once they become qualified to do so. According to Zeleza, the number of African immigrants acquiring U.S. citizenship increased from 7,122 in 1988 to 21,842 in 1996. [20]

Altogether, about 108,441 Africans became naturalized citizens during this period. A major reason why an increasing number of Africans are acquiring United States citizenship rather than remaining just permanent residents with a green card is because many of them have finally reconciled themselves to the fact that the United States is home and that they are here to stay. Additionally, the acquisition of citizenship allows them to participate in the political process, thereby giving them a voice, albeit a small one, in the political decision-making process in the local, state and national government.

Living the American Dream

Although African immigrants can be found in many small towns and cities throughout the United States, major cities like New York, Chicago, Minneapolis, Los Angeles, Houston, Dallas, Atlanta, Boston, and the Washington D.C. area continue to attract the largest number of immigrants.

It is estimated that in 2000, 1 percent or 92,435 of the population of New York City were African-born immigrants, while Montgomery experienced a 15 percent increase to 25,776 in the number of African immigrants in the 1990s. [21] Similarly, there were about 200,000 African immigrants in Atlanta in 2003. [22]

These cities remain magnets for African immigrants because of the presence of friends and relatives who are able to provide temporary residence for the new immigrants until they are able to situate themselves. Another advantage of living with these acquaintances, albeit on a temporary basis is the fact that they also provide the new immigrants with important advice on surviving in the United States.

Increasingly, the quest for areas where the immigrants can live is influenced by the immigrant's desire to live a more tranquil life and raise their children in safer environments than can be provided in some of the larger cities like New York, Chicago, Houston or Los Angeles.

But perhaps the most important factor influencing the decision to migrate to any particular city or area is the prevailing racial climate, political tolerance toward immigrants, and employment opportunities. That may explain why Atlanta, where Blacks occupy important economic and political positions in the city administration has become a Mecca for African immigrants. [23]

Often, these immigrants are quick to take any employment opportunity that they can get. Although there were about 100,000 highly educated African professionals throughout the United States in 1999, [24] many more are also involved in jobs where less education and often less skill may be required. They work as cab drivers, parking lot attendants, airport workers or waiters, waitresses, and cooks in restaurants. Still others have become entrepreneurs.

In Washington D.C., New York, Atlanta, Los Angeles, Houston and Miami, for example, African immigrants own restaurants, healthcare agencies and specialty stores that cater to the needs of the large African and other immigrant population in these cities.

Even African women who have traditionally been in the background of most traditional African family structure now find themselves at the forefront of economic opportunities in the United States and thus are playing important economic roles in maintaining the family structure both for the family members who are still in Africa and those in the United States. Commenting on the importance of African women immigrants to the United States, Daff reminds us that African women, especially those from West Africa have stopped waiting for their men to mail checks home from the United States and have joined them, earning their own income, while others have been coming alone, leaving husbands and children behind. [25]

With a median income of over $40,000 in 2003, [26] many African immigrants are not only expected to support their families in the United States, but also other relatives back in Africa. In his 1991 study for example, Apraku noted that 37 percent of his respondents remitted between $1,500 and $3,000, while 20 percent sent between $3,000 to more than $10,000 annually to support friends and relatives back in their home countries. [27]

While these amounts may not be significant to an average middle class American, they are of vital importance in continent, and to a people where a few hundred dollars might determine whether a parent lives or dies, or whether a sibling continues to attend school or not.

The new African immigrant is no longer just interested in making money they are also interested in building stronger communities and organizing themselves in order to become a more powerful political and economic force in their respective communities.

Groups such as the All African Peoples Organization in Omaha, Nebraska, the Nigerian-American Chamber of Commerce in Miami, the Tristate (Ohio, Indiana and Kentucky) Cameroon Family, the Nigerian Women Eagles Club in Cincinnati, Ohio, and the African Heritage Inc. in Wisconsin all aim to help their members become active in their communities and create a better understanding between Africans and Americans.

Some Africans point to the tremendous influence of the Cuban community in Miami as a blueprint for what Africans in cities like Atlanta, Chicago, Houston and Minneapolis can accomplish if they are well organized.

Despite their dedication, hard work and determination to realize the American dream, African immigrants are often faced with the reality of what Aman calls the "innocence about race relations" [28] that they had left Africa with as they struggle to make a living in their new homeland.

First, they encounter some of the same stereotypes often associated with their African American counterparts. [29] They are often perceived as lazy, criminals, drug dealers and welfare cheats. This perception often results in police harassment, intimidation, unlawful arrests and even murder.

In fact, the February 1999 killing by New York police officers of Amadou Diallo, an African immigrant from Guinea near his home in the Bronx has become a metaphor for the way African immigrants are perceived and treated by some law enforcement authorities.

Uwah, for instance, questions why successful African immigrants like himself, who have all the right American values of hard work, and education, and have embraced assimilation into the mainstream culture are still not accepted like other immigrants from Europe, Cuba or Asia who also possess those same values or are even less enterprising. [30]

Another problem faced by African immigrants is the lack of acceptance by some of their African American counterparts. African immigrants are perceived by some African Americans as responsible for the fact that their ancestors were sold into slavery. There is also the accusation that African immigrants see themselves as better, if not superior to their African American counterparts. [31]

Unfortunately, this perception has led to an uneasy relationship between some African immigrants and their African American brothers and sisters that continue to divide and paralyze Blacks in America thereby making them ineffective political and economic forces in national politics.

Conclusion and Observation

This paper has focused on how the breakdown of the post-colonial economy and the collapse of viable political institutions have contributed to the significant increase in the number of African immigrants to the United States, especially since the early 1980s.

Unlike their counterparts of the 1960s and 70s, whose primary objective was to obtain an American education before returning home to contribute to the task of nation-building, the "new" immigrants are mainly refugees and asylum seekers escaping the ravages of civil wars and political persecution in their homelands, or highly skilled professionals disappointed by the worsening economic situation in many African states.

Also unlike their early counterparts, these "new" immigrants come with every intention of establishing permanent residency and acquiring United States citizenship. Consequently, they are fast learning how to live the American dream; they are becoming involved in their communities, starting small businesses, and participating in local politics.

Their children are becoming professional football, baseball and basketball players. They are also becoming highly trained professionals who are employed in both the public and private sectors. What the future holds for the continued flow of African migration to the United States is unclear.

But from all indications it appears that African migration, immigration, and integration into American political, social and economic spheres will continue.

The continuous proliferation of civil wars across the continent- Liberia, Sierra Leone, Côte d'Ivoire and the Democratic Republic of Congo- is not a positive sign for a continent where nearly half a century ago the prospect of independence was greeted with tremendous optimism and great expectations.

Endnotes

[1] Medrano N. Leslie, "Immigration: Africans Find They Have Everything Here'; Minnesota Has Become a Migratory Hub for Some groups&" *Star Tribune*, June 4, 2002.

[2] Rob Carson, "African Immigrants at 172-year High" *The News Tribune*, January 5, 2003.

[3] Soumana Sako, "Brain Drain and Africa's Development: A Reflection" *African Issues*, 30 (1), 2002, p. 28.

[4] Kaye Whiteman, "The Gallic Paradox" *Africa Report*, January/February 1991, p. 19.

[5] Kofi K. Apraku, *African Émigrés in the United States*, New York: Praeger Publishers, 1991, p. 82.

[6] Olusegun Obasanjo, "Africa in the 1990s: The Challenge of Economic Reform" in Olusegun Obasanjo and Hans d'Orville, (eds.), *The Leadership Challenge of Economic Reforms in Africa*, New York: Crane Russack, pp. 1-11.

[7] Ahmad Abubakar, *Africa and the Challenge of Development: Acquiescence and Dependency versus Freedom and Development*, New York: Praeger Publishers, 1989, p. 27.

[8] "Nigeria: Where Does it Go From Here?" *West Africa*, October 4-10, 1993, p. 1760.

[9] George S. Dei and Asgharzadeh Alireza, "What is to be Done?: A Look at Some Causes and Consequences of the African Brain Drain" *African Issues*, 30 (1), 2002, p. 32.

[10] James Butty, "Dream or Drain?" *West Africa*, March 4-10, 1991, p. 295.

[11] Cited in Soumana Sako, "Brain Drain and Africa's Development: A Reflection," *African Issues*, XXX(1), 2002, p. 26.

[12] Joseph Takougang, "Recent African Immigrants to the United States: A Historical Perspective." *The Western Journal of Black Studies*, 19(1). Also see, Kinuthia Macharia, "The Truth- Students who have Returned and those Who Won't" *The East African Standard*, February 17, 2003.

[13] Kinuthia Macharia, "The Truth- Students who have Returned and those Who Won't" *The East Africa Standard*, February 17, 2003.

[15] George S. Dei and Asgharzadeh Alireza, "What is to be Done? A Look at Some Causes and Consequences of the African Brain Drain" *African Issues*, 30 (1), 2002. p. 33.

[16] See, for example, Halimah Adbullah, "African Immigrants Defer Dreams of Returning Home" *The Dallas Morning News*, April 2, 1999; John A. Arthur, *Invisible Sojourners: African Immigrant Diaspora in the United States*, Westport, CT: Praeger Publishers, 2000; Rob Carson, "African Immigrations at 172-year High" *The News Tribune*, January 5, 2003.

[17] Paul T. Zeleza, "Contemporary African Migration in a Global Context" *African Issues* 30 (1), 2002, p. 13; Yanki K. Djamba, "African Immigrants to the United States: A Socio-Demographic Profile in Comparison to Native Blacks" *Journal of*

Asian and African Studies 34(2), 1999.

[18] Paul T. Zeleza, "Contemporary African Migration in a Global Context" *African Issues* 30 (1), 2002, p. 14.

[19] Cited by Marieme Daff, "Women-Migration: Women Taking their Places in African Immigration" *Inter Press Services*, August 9, 2002. Some Senegalese immigrants in the city estimate that the number might be as high as 30,000.

[20] Paul T. Zeleza, "Contemporary African Migration in a Global Context" *African Issues* 30 (1), 2002, p.12.

[21] David Snyder, "Signs of a Boom in African Influx: Surge's Impact Seen Throughout Country" *The Washington Post*, July 11, 2002.

[22] Rick Bodie, "Entrepreneurial Spirit Brings Africans Here: Growth Points to Bright Future" *The Atlanta Journal Constitution*, March 9, 2003.

[23] *The Florida Times*, May 7, 2000.

[24] *Africa News Service*, November 21, 1999.

[25] Marieme Daff, "Women-Migration: Women Taking Their Places in African Immigration" *Inter Press services*, August 9, 2002.

[26] Cindy Rodriguez, "Study Shows US Blacks Trailing Immigrants from Africa, Caribbean" *The Boston Globe*, February 17, 2003.

[27] Kofi K. Apraku, *African Émigrés in the United States*, New York: Praeger Publishers, 1991, p. 6.

[28] Mohammed Aman, "Foreword" in Obiakor Festus E and Grant Patrick A (eds.), *Foreign-Born African Americans: Silenced Voices in the Discourse on Race*, New York: Nova Science Publishers, Inc. 2002, p. xiii.

[29] Njubi F. Nesbitt, "African Intellectuals in the Belly of the Beast: Migration, Identity and the Politics of Exile" *African Issues*, 30 (I), p. 71.

[30] George O. Uwah , "Reflections of an African-Born Immigrant: Story of Alienation" in Obiakor E. Festus and Patrick A. Grant, (eds.), *Foreign-Born African Americans: Silenced Voices in the Discourse on Race*, New York: Nova Science Publishers, Inc. 2002. Also see other chapters in the book for an excellent discussion of some of the problems faced by African immigrants.

[31] My personal observation is that it is not a matter of African immigrants seeing themselves as superior to their African American counterparts or vice versa. Rather, like with other immigrant groups- Irish versus Italians, English versus Irish etc.- it is an issue of deep-seated cultural differences with neither side often unwilling to acknowledge those differences and working through them.

References

Adbullah, Halimah "African Immigrants Defer Dreams of Returning Home" *The Dallas Morning News*, April 2, 1999.

Abubakar, Ahmad *Africa and the Challenge of Development: Acquiescence and Dependency versus Freedom and Development*, New York: Praeger Publishers, 1989.

Africa News Service, November 21, 1999.

Aman, Mohammed "Foreword" in Obiakor, Festus E. and Patrick A Grant, (eds.), *Foreign-Born African Americans: Silenced Voices in the Discourse on Race*, New York: Nova Science Publishers, Inc. 2002

Apraku, Kofi K. *African Émigrés in the United States*, New York: Praeger Publishers, 1991, p. 82.

Arthur, John A. *Invisible Sojourners: African Immigrant Diaspora in the United States*, Westport, CT: Praeger Publishers, 2000.

Bodie, Rick "Entrepreneurial Spirit Brings Africans here: Growth Points to Bright Future" *The Atlanta Journal Constitution*, March 9, 2003.

Butty, James "Dream or Drain?" *West Africa*, March 4-10, 1991, p. 295.

Carson, Rob "African Immigrants at 172-year High" *The News Tribune*, January 5, 2003.

Daff, Marieme "Women-Migration: Women Taking Their Places in African Immigration" *Inter Press Services*, August 9, 2002. Some Senegalese immigrants in the city estimate that the number might be as high as 30,000.

Djamba, Yanki K. "African Immigrants to the United States: A Socio-Demographic Profile in Comparison to Native Blacks" *Journal of Asian and African Studies* 34(2), 1999.

Dei, George S. and Alireza Asgharzadeh. "What is to be done?

A Look at Some Causes and Consequences of the African Brain Drain" *African Issues*, 30 (1), 2002, p. 32.

The Florida Times, May 7, 2000.

Leslie, Medrano N. "Immigration: Africans Find They Have Everything Here'; Minnesota Has Become a Migratory Hub for Some Groups&" *Star Tribune*, June 4, 2002.

Macharia, Kinuthia "The Truth - Students Who Have Returned and Those Who Won't" *The East African Standard*, February 17, 2003.

Nesbitt, Njubi F. "African Intellectuals in the Belly of the Beast: Migration, Identity and the Politics of Exile" *African Issues*, 30 (I).

"Nigeria: Where Does it Go From Here?" *West Africa*, October 4-10, 1993.

Obasanjo, Olusegun "Africa in the 1990s: The Challenge of Economic Reform" in Olusegun Obasanjo and Hans d'Orville, (eds.)*The Leadership Challenge of Economic Reforms in Africa*, New York: Crane Russack, pp. 1-11.

Rodriguez, Cindy "Study Shows US Blacks Trailing Immigrants from Africa, Caribbean" *The Boston Globe*, February 17, 2003.

Sako, Soumana "Brain Drain and Africa's Development: A Reflection" *African Issues*, 30 (1), 2002, p. 28.

Snyder, David "Signs of a Boom in African Influx: Surge's Impact Seen Throughout Country" *The Washington Post*, July 11, 2002.

Takougang, Joseph "Recent African Immigrants to the United States: A Historical Perspective" *The Western Journal of Black Studies*, 19(1).

Uwah, George O. "Reflections of an African-Born Immigrant: Story of Alienation" in Obiakor E. Festus and Grant A. Patrick A. (eds.), *Foreign-Born African Americans: Silenced Voices in the Discourse on Race*, New York: Nova Science Publishers, Inc. 2002.

Whiteman, Kaye "The Gallic Paradox" *Africa Report*, January/February 1991, p. 19.

Zeleza, Paul T. "Contemporary African Migration in a Global Context" *African Issues* 30 (1), 2002.

Joseph Takougang is an Associate Professor of African history in the Department of African American Studies at the University of Cincinnati, Cincinnati, Ohio, USA.

Appendix III:

Afro-Caribbeans in Britain

THE British African-Caribbean (Afro-Caribbean) community are residents of the United Kingdom who are of West Indian background, and whose ancestors were indigenous to Africa.

As immigration to the United Kingdom from Africa increased in the 1990s, the term has been used to include UK residents solely of African origin, or as a term to define all Black British residents, though this is usually denoted by "African *and* Caribbean".

The most common and traditional use of the term Afro-Caribbean community is in reference to groups of residents continuing aspects of Caribbean culture, customs and traditions in the United Kingdom.

The largest proportion of the African-Caribbean population in the UK are of Jamaican origin.

Others trace origins to smaller nations including Trinidad and Tobago, Saint Kitts and Nevis, Barbados, Saint Lucia, Grenada, Montserrat, Dominica, Anguilla, Antigua and Barbuda, Saint Vincent and the Grenadines; Guyana, which though located on the South American mainland, has close cultural ties to the Caribbean, and was historically considered to be part of the British West Indies; and Belize (formerly British Honduras), in Central America, which culturally is more akin to the Caribbean than to Latin America, due to its colonial and still-extant economic ties to the UK.

African-Caribbean communities exist throughout the United Kingdom, though by far the largest concentrations are in London,

Birmingham and the broader West Midlands conurbation.

Significant communities also exist in other population centres, notably Manchester, Nottingham, Leicester, Bristol, Leeds, Sheffield, Liverpool and Cardiff.

In these cities the community is traditionally associated with a particular area, such as Chapeltown in Leeds or St. Pauls in Bristol.

History

African-Caribbeans are primarily the descendants of West Africans captured or obtained in trade from African procurers. The Africans were then shipped by European slave traders to English, French, Dutch, Spanish, and Portuguese colonies founded from the 16th century. On arrival, the majority of Africans were set to work on the vast Caribbean sugar plantations for the benefit of the colonial powers.

Migration from the Caribbean to Britain was rare before World War II, and little is known about the experiences of those who made the move. There are records of small communities in the ports of Cardiff, Liverpool and South Shields dating back to the mid-19th century.

These communities were formed by freed slaves following the abolition of slavery. Typical occupations of the early migrants were footmen or coachmen, though a growing Caribbean presence in the British military led to approximately 15,000 migrants arriving in the North-West of England around the time of the First World War to work in munitions factories.

Since World War II many African-Caribbeans migrated to North America and Europe, especially to the United States, Canada, the UK, and the Netherlands.

As a result of the losses during the war, the British government began to encourage mass immigration from the countries of the British Empire and Commonwealth to fill shortages in the labour market.

The 1948 British Nationality Act gave British citizenship to all people living in Commonwealth countries, and full rights of entry and settlement in Britain. Many West Indians were attracted by better prospects in what was often referred to as the mother country.

The "Windrush generation"

The ship *Empire Windrush* brought the first group of 492 immigrants to Tilbury near London on 22 June 1948. The *Windrush* was en route from Australia to England via the Atlantic, docking in Kingston, Jamaica. An advert had appeared in a Jamaican newspaper offering cheap transport on the ship for anybody who wanted to come and work in the UK. The arrivals were temporarily housed in the Clapham South deep shelter in southwest London less than a mile away from Coldharbour Lane in Brixton.

Many only intended to stay in Britain for a few years, and although a number returned to the Caribbean to rejoin the RAF (Royal Air Force), the majority remained to settle permanently.

The arrival of the passengers has become an important landmark in the history of modern Britain, and the image of the Caribbeans filing off its gangplank has come to symbolise the beginning of modern British multicultural society.

There was plenty of work in post-war Britain and industries such as British Rail, the National Health Service and public transport recruited almost exclusively from Jamaica and Barbados.

Though African-Caribbeans were encouraged to journey to Britain via immigration campaigns created by successive British governments, many new arrivals were to endure intolerance and extreme racism from certain sectors of indigenous British society. This experience was to mark African-Caribbeans' relations with the wider community over a long period.

Early African-Caribbean immigrants found private employment and housing denied to them on the basis of race. Housing was in short supply following the wartime bombing, and the shortage led to some of the first clashes with the established white community.

Clashes continued and worsened into the 1950s, and riots erupted in cities including London, Birmingham and Nottingham.

In 1958, attacks in the London area of Notting Hill by white youths marred relations with West Indian residents, leading to the creation of the annual Notting Hill Carnival, which was initiated in 1959 as a positive response by the Caribbean community.

In 1962, Britain passed the Commonwealth Immigrants Act restricting the entry of immigrants, and by 1972 only holders of work permits, or people with parents or grandparents born in the UK could gain entry - effectively stemming most Caribbean immigration.

Despite the restrictive measures, an entire generation of Britons with African-Caribbean heritage now existed, contributing to British society in virtually every field. The number of British persons born in the West Indies had increased from 15,000 in 1951 to 172,000 in 1961 to 304,000 in 1981. The total population of persons of West Indian heritage by 1981 was between 500,000 and 550,000, depending upon the official source used.

Recession and turbulence, 1970s and 1980s

The 1970s and 1980s were decades of comparative turbulence in wider British society; industrial disputes preceded a period of deep recession and widespread unemployment which seriously affected the economically less prosperous African-Caribbean community.

Perceived societal racism, discrimination, poverty, powerlessness and oppressive policing sparked a series of riots in areas with substantial African-Caribbean populations.

These "uprisings" (as they were described by some in the community) took place in St Pauls in 1980, Brixton, Toxteth and Moss Side in 1981, St Pauls again in 1982, Notting Hill Gate in 1982, Toxteth in 1982, and Handsworth, Brixton and Tottenham in 1985.

The riots had a profoundly unsettling effect on local residents, and led the then Home Secretary William Whitelaw to commission the Scarman Report to address the root causes of the disturbances.

The report identified both "racial discrimination" and a "racial disadvantage" in Britain, concluding that urgent action was needed to prevent these issues becoming an "endemic, ineradicable disease threatening the very survival of our society." The era saw an increase in attacks on Black people by white people. The *Joint Campaign Against Racism* committee reported that there had been more than 20,000 attacks on non-indigenous Britons including Britons of Asian origin during 1985.

Recent history

While individuals with Caribbean heritage excelled in a variety of fields in British society during the 1990s and 2000s, many recurring issues continued to impact the African-Caribbean community as a whole.

The police response to the 1993 murder of Black teenager Stephen Lawrence, by assailants that have yet to be convicted, led to an outcry from the community and calls to investigate police conduct. The subsequent government inquiry, the Macpherson Report, was vigorously sought by Stephen's Jamaican-born parents and revealed evidence of institutional racism in the London Metropolitan Police Service, confirming the beliefs of many Black Britons.

The community has suffered from an increasing association with gun-crime, heightened by high profile murders, such as that of two young women shot outside a Birmingham hair salon in 2003.

Several media outlets blamed a "gangster rap culture" in the community, though Assistant Chief Constable Nick Tofiluk of the West Midlands Police believed that the use of firearms is not an Afro-Caribbean issue alone, and has been on the rise throughout British society.

Tensions between African-Caribbean residents and British Asians in a number of regions have led to confrontations, notably violent disturbances in Birmingham in 2005 where groups from both communities fought and rioted over two nights.

There is also evidence of tensions between the African-Caribbean community and the growing number of African immigrants.

Source: *Wikipedia*, 2007.

About the Author

Godfrey Mwakikagile comes from Tanzania. He has written a number of books mostly about Africa. He has also written some books about the United States focusing on Black America

They include *Nyerere and Africa: End of an Era*; *Africa After Independence: Realities of Nationhood*; *Relations Between Africans and African Americans: Misconceptions, Myths and Realities*; and *Africa and America in The Sixties: A Decade That Changed The Nation and The Destiny of A Continent.*

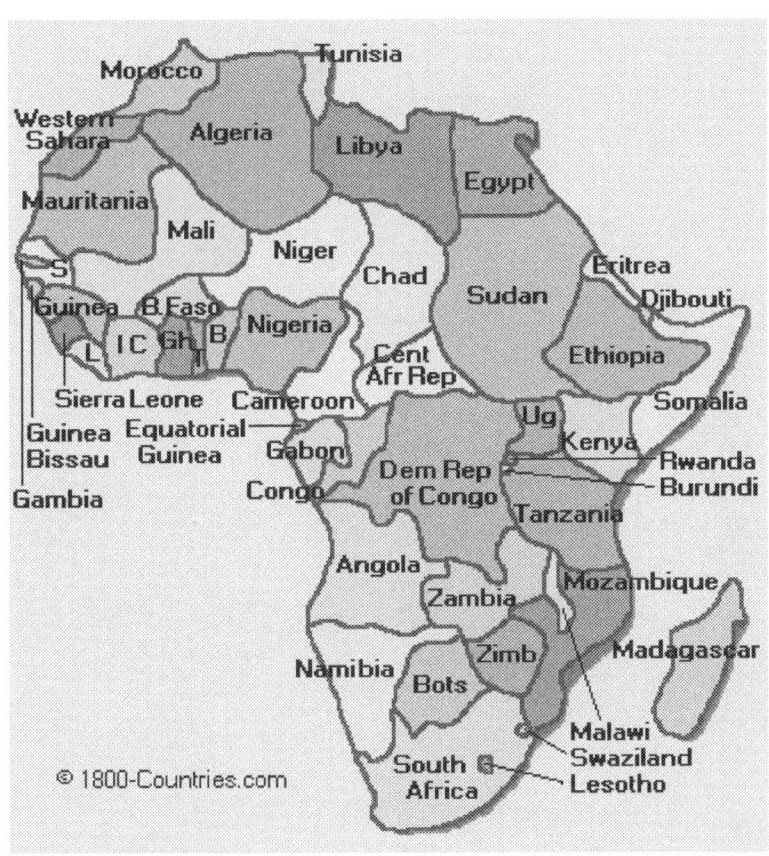

Lightning Source UK Ltd.
Milton Keynes UK
UKHW042040291122
413043UK00001B/206